JENNIFER ROWLEY

STRATEGIC MANAGEMENT INFORMATION SYSTEMS AND TECHNIQUES

BLACKWELL
Manchester and Oxford

First published 1994

First published in USA 1994

Blackwell Publishers
108 Cowley Road
Oxford OX4 1JF
UK

283 Main Street
Cambridge, Massachusetts 02142
USA

Editorial Office: NCC Blackwell Ltd, Oxford House,
Oxford Road, Manchester M1 7ED

ISBN 1-85554-210-2

Library of Congress data is available

Typeset in 10.5 on 12pt Times Roman by ScribeTech Ltd, Bradford
Printed and bound in Great Britain by Hartnolls Limited, Bodmin, Cornwall

This book is printed on acid-free paper

Preface

Aim

This book reviews the basics of decision theory and a number of techniques that might be applied in strategic decision making. The techniques are reviewed in the context of the management information systems that provide the data with which these techniques might be used and often offer the facilities for ready application of these techniques.

The book is addressed to the manager as a *user* of management information systems and not as a *manager* of such systems. It focuses on the ways in which management information and systems can be exploited in order to support effective decision making. Increasingly many managers will interact with information systems in both roles, but existing textbooks on management information systems tend to consider the design of such systems alone. Other textbooks deal separately with decision theory or decision making techniques. This book also recognises that an understanding of decision theory and its techniques in isolation from an appreciation of the information and information systems on which the analysis is performed, can prove extremely misleading.

The other demands on most managers' time mean that many managers spend only a short time acquainting themselves with the nature and potential of management information systems, whether they encounter such systems in their working environment, or whilst they are involved in management education. This text, then, distills key concepts and techniques, and presents them in a format which is easy to assimilate. The text is not comprehensive, but offers a framework upon which the manager may build a wider knowledge, of and experience with, management information systems.

Audience

This book is written for managers and those who need to study management information systems on management and business studies courses. It is particularly appropriate for post experience courses such as Diploma in Management Studies, M.Sc in Management Studies, and MBA courses.

Structure

The first chapter identifies the role of management information systems and decision making techniques in strategic decision making. Part One, then, goes on to explore different kinds of information systems in detail. Chapters in Part One consider Management information, Management Information Systems, Decision support systems and other types of Management Information Systems. Part Two looks at a range of fundamental concepts associated with model building and decision making under uncertainty. The focus is on the basic concepts of model building, decision criteria, decision trees, and utility. A range of other model building techniques are reviewed in the concluding chapter.

Each chapter concludes with a short list of review questions and some short case study examples for the reader to reflect upon. The review questions are intended to encourage you to assess whether you have assimilated what you have just read. The case study examples ask you to apply the techniques and concepts in a controlled way, as a prerequisite to applying them in your own working or study environment.

Acknowledgments

Many people have contributed to the creation of this book and I am indebted to all of them. Specifically I should like to thank John Douglas and Peter Rowley for their comments on an earlier draft of the manuscript and my family Peter, Shula and Zeta for their patience during the busy time associated with the writing of this book.

Jennifer Rowley, July 1993.

Contents

Part 2

Part I

I

Management and Decision Making

Objectives

When you have read this chapter you will:
- have an appreciation of the scope of the book as a whole;
- understand the definition of a strategic management information system;
- be aware of the roles of different levels of management in the decision making process;
- appreciate the complexity of the decision making process;
- appreciate the need for data in the decision making process.

Management Information Systems - Some Definitions

The term management information systems (MIS) can be used to mean different things by different authors, and indeed it is not unusual to encounter more than one definition in one book! Books on management information systems vary in their emphasis from a very hardware/software based approach to an approach that views the MIS as a means of processing data into information, which is then used for decision making. Here, we are concerned with the way in which the MIS provides information for management activities. Two complementary definitions offered by other authors are appropriate in defining the perspective offered in this book.

Lucey describes an MIS as

A system to convert data from internal and external sources into information and to communicate that information, in an appropriate form, to managers at all levels in all functions to enable them to make timely and effective decisions for planning, directing and controlling the activities for which they are responsible.

Senn offers a complementary definition:

An MIS is an integrated system for providing information to support the planning, control, and operations of an organisation. It aids operations, management and decision making by providing past-, present- and future- oriented information about internal operations and external intelligence. It provides information in a timely fashion.

An MIS, is then, any system that provides information for the management activities carried out within an organisation. Nowadays the term is almost exclusively reserved for computerised systems. These consist of hardware and software which accept data and store, process and retrieve information. This information is selected and presented in a form suitable for managerial decision making and for the planning and monitoring of the organisations activities.

Strategies

This book uses the term Strategic Management Information Systems or SMIS. Why do we describe MIS as Strategic? In order to answer this question it is necessary to explore the concept of strategic or strategies.

Managers set **organisational objectives,** and then determine a **strategy** to accomplish those objectives. They then organise the organisation's **resources** in order to execute those strategies.

> A system or application may be described as **strategic** if it changes the way that an organisation competes.

A strategy is the way in which an organisation endeavours to differentiate itself from its competitors, using its relative corporate strengths to meet customer needs better. A strategy is successful if it ensures a better or stronger matching of corporate strengths to customer needs than is provided by its competitors. This concept is grounded in the three interacting components: the *corporation* in relation to its *customers* and its *competitors*. An effective management strategist is able to achieve superior performance whilst making sure that the chosen strategy matches the strengths of the organisation with the needs of the customer. See Figure 1.1.

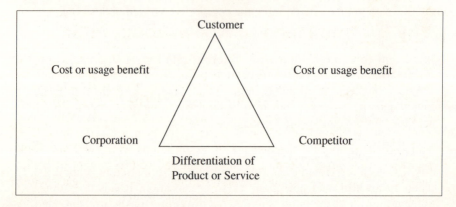

Figure 1.1 Elements in the Strategic Triangle

Managers are increasingly recognising the competitive and strategic value of information systems. Of all of the assets of an organisation, including personnel, financial capital, plant and equipment, information is by far the most valuable, because it describes these physical resources and the environment in which they exist. The possession of physical resources without information about them is of little use. Information about the resources is essential if these resources are to be used effectively. In many organisations there is a shift in the role of information systems from that of *supporting* the business to *being* the business. Increasingly, managers will seek business value from investment in information systems. Information must be used to support the organisation's objectives if it is to have any value. Information may be used strategically to, for instance, create competitive advantage, alter the competitive balance between companies, change the nature of industries and to generate new business for many organisations.

The new role of information systems give rise to five key issues:

- Information systems must be aligned with the organisation's objectives.
- Strategic information systems, both within and between organisations will increasingly shape and support the competitive strategy of the organisation and influence internal activities.
- The benefits from the organisation's investment in information systems will be monitored more closely, and new procedures for assessing the economic benefit of developing and using information systems are emerging.
- Evaluation of the exposure to risk from information systems failure will be more essential.
- It will be increasingly necessary to assess and monitor the extent to which information systems conform to government regulations and corporate policy.

> All information systems should be strategic, that is, they should all have an effect on the organisation's competitive position.

Why Do You Need to Know About MIS?

The extent of use of MIS and the extent to which MIS are structured varies considerably between different organisations. This book seeks to offer a perspective that is relevant to all managers, whatever their working environment. In order to achieve this, it will in places be necessary to make elementary observations. These may be news to the manager in the less MIS-oriented organisation. Even managers in organisations where MIS are well integrated often benefit from a re-statement and re-assessment of basic principles. Whatever the organisational environment, every manager should be familiar with the MIS in their organisation and be able to take a critical view of their development. Managers need to know about MIS because:

- MIS are fundamental tools for problem solving and decision making, and if you do not make effective use of these tools as a decision maker, the quality of your decisions may be impaired.
- Managers are affected by others who use MIS. The characteristics of the MIS, and the way in which your colleagues use the MIS may have significant impact on your working life.
- Managers should participate in and influence MIS design and use so that MIS need their needs.
- Managers should be able to recognise when the MIS available to them in their organisation are ineffective.

Strategic Management Information Systems

Evidence from the UK and the USA suggests that existing MIS often have limited success in providing management with the information that it needs. MIS design presents many problems and some of these are inherent and will always challenge the systems designer, but others arise from insufficient involvement of management in the design of MIS systems.

Amongst the factors that will always need to be addressed by MIS design and which will present challenges are:

- Different managers have different information needs.
- Changes in the environment can trigger significant change in the information requirements of individual managers.
- Some management decisions are more structured than others.
- Management decisions have different levels of predictability.
- Managers have different decision making approaches and styles.

Given these inherent problems, it is important to start to resolve some of the other issues. It has been suggested that MIS are not as effective as they might be because there is:

- lack of management involvement with the design of MIS;
- lack of management appreciation of information requirements and the potential of MIS to meet these requirements;
- lack of knowledge by information specialists of management;
- undue concentration on transaction processing systems;
- lack of top management support for MIS.

All of these problems must be addressed if an MIS is to have a key strategic role. Experience has shown that MIS must be designed and operated with due regard to organisational objectives. Management must be able and willing to make an effective contribution to systems design and information systems specialists must become more aware of managerial functions.

Management Functions and Levels

There is a temptation to go straight to existing MIS and to examine their nature. It is more appropriate to review the basic activities of management and to assess the information that might be required to meet these needs, as a basis for considering the effectiveness of MIS.

Managers fulfil a wide variety of different roles within an organisation and each of these roles may generate a requirement for information. Management functions are often categorised into planning, organising, staffing, controlling and communicating.
These involve:

- Planning, or establishing goals and developing policies, procedures and programs to achieve these goals;
- Organising, or grouping activities and establishing organisational structures and procedures so that activities are performed;
- Staffing, including obtaining and training personnel to work in the organisation in order to achieve goals and objectives;
- Communicating, as in for example, transferring information on goals, objectives and performance to personnel throughout the organisation and the environment;
- Elucidating information, including identifying the most appropriate information and applying it to a situation.

Managers have a different span of control in relation to these activities depending on their responsibilities These can be broadly categorised by identifying three levels of management. In most organisations management roles can be organised into three levels:

Top or strategic management which performs planning and strategy formulation activities. This level of management is oriented towards the future of the organisation and oversees the performance of a few key people who execute the plans. Planning for the future is a primary role, and responsibilities involve co-ordination and liaison with external organisations.

Middle or tactical management is concerned with overseeing the performance of the organisation . This includes monitoring the extent to which objectives are being met, and controlling those activities that move the organisation in the direction of its goals. Managers at this level are concerned with issues such as personnel training and other personnel considerations, and equipment and materials acquisition.

Operational management are concerned with the day-to-day operation of the activities of the organisation. Primary concerns are schedules, deadlines, human relations and cost and quality control.

In a more traditional and hierarchically structured organisation these roles may coincide with posts, and people, but it is often the case that managers have roles that have elements of more than one of these levels. Managers in smaller organisations, especially, are likely to have responsibilities that extend across all levels of management. Accordingly, the manager will exhibit an information requirements profile that reflects the range of their responsibilities. Whilst we shall use these three roles in order to structure our comments concerning information needs and the use of information systems by managers, it is important to recognise that managerial structures and roles differ between organisations, and that management information systems must be designed in the light of the management roles in a given organisation.

An example might help to clarify the roles of these different levels of management. Consider the issue of marketing policies for the organisation's main products or services. Strategic managers identify the most important aspects of the marketing effort such as advertising, pricing, product quality, packaging, transportation, distribution, and establish policies to address each aspect. At middle management level, the policies that top management formulates are developed in greater detail. In this example, a typical activity might be establishing advertising programmes. These programmes will include a statement of the message that is to encourage customers and potential customers to buy the product or to keep buying the product. The message may emphasise the product characteristics most likely to sell the product, such as price, quality and style.

Once the advertising programmes are outlined, operational managers determine exactly where adverts are to be placed, by selecting newspapers and magazines and deciding when advertisements will appear. Any broadcast media that will carry the advertisements have daily and long term schedules for airing them. Similar programmes will be developed by other managers to execute management policies on transportation, packaging and other areas.

Since information is key to many management activities more efficient processing of information, more effective identification of relevant information, and the presentation of information in formats that are easy to assimilate has a significant impact on the management structure of many organisations, leading often to a reduction in the number of levels of management.

Managerial Use of Information

Managers use information for planning and control activities, as well as those activities concerned with the production of goods and services. These activities include decision making, reporting and the use of information in the product or service.

Planning and Control

Planning precedes any activity in an organisation. In planning, objectives are defined, strategies to achieve those objectives are selected and the resources necessary to implement the actions are determined. Success is the result of a strategic plan that meets the objectives defined by the top management. Planning is also undertaken by managers at tactical and operational levels; here plans are based on the strategic plan.

Control activities direct actions through the planning process. This is achieved through budgets, standards and other performance criteria. The control process includes feedback that serves to compare the results of the action with the planned outcome. Many reports and other information are used in planning and control.

Decision Making

Information is necessary to support decision making. The nature of the information depends on the type of decision and the organisational level at which a decision is made. The use of information in management decision making is explored more fully in the next section.

Reporting

Outside parties may require reports from an information system. For example, regulatory bodies may require reports on the number of accidents or the emissions produced by a manufacturing process. Tax authorities require payroll tax information and shareholders require annual reports. Information systems must generate such reports.

Product and Service Information

Information may be an integral component of the product or service that an organisation provides to its customers. For example, many software suppliers maintain a customer file so that they can offer them a better service by informing them of modifications and upgrades.

The Decision Making Process

One of the central management activities is decision making. Decision making is concerned with recognising problems, generating alternative solutions to the problem, choosing from amongst the alternatives , and implementing the chosen alternative. Since decision making is central to management, the designer of an MIS must take into account the nature of the decision making process. Several types of MIS have been developed to accommodate the different types of decisions.

This book focuses on the use of management information systems in decision making. An exploration of the activities associated with decision making would form a sound basis for consideration of the role of MIS in decision making. First, we define a decision :

> A decision is the selection of a specific course of action or solution from a set of possible alternative courses of action.

Decisions are often made more difficult by **uncertainty** which makes it difficult to be sure which course of action or strategy will lead to the best outcome. Ignorance which derives from the failure of the manager to assimilate and/or understand the available data can contribute to uncertainty.

Because decision making is a key, but complex, activity theorists have tried to explain how organisations and individuals make decisions.

Some decisions are routine or structured. For example, sales order processing and the approval of customer credit occur sufficiently often to be routine and for systems and procedures to be developed to handle decisions in these areas. It is easy to identify the relevant factors to consider when deciding whether to accept an order or to approve credit. Determining whether to launch a new product or close a plant is a non-routine, unstructured decision making situation. Clear cut procedures rarely exist to cater for these situations. Some decisions are semi-structured in that it is possible to identify some of the relevant factors and data may be available to allow the decision maker to assess some factors, but other factors are less straightforward to identify.

> All decision making processes can be viewed as having eight steps:
>
> - Establish a single unambiguous objective against which to evaluate any outcome, and thereby define the problem. Typical examples might be: to maximize profit, to minimise costs, or to maximize quality of service.
> - State the objective in numeric or financial terms having gathered appropriate data to be able to do so.
> - Select a set of possible alternative strategies for consideration. This step can only consider those alternative strategies that are known, and therefore assumes that all alternatives are known.
> - Determine and build the model to be used to represent the strategies in terms of the objective, and identify the values (measures) of the parameters in the process.
> - Rank the alternatives.
> - Determine which strategy optimises or gives the best value for the objective established in step 1. Choose this course of action for adoption.
> - Implement the chosen strategy.
> - Monitor the success of the strategy.

There is a general flow through the eight steps, but the process should be viewed as iterative and return to an earlier phase should be expected from time to time. Few decisions are taken in a neat logical sequence. Feedback, the inter-relationships between distinct decisions, intuition, judgement and creativity all make a contribution to effective decision making and ensure that decision making is a complex process.

Information is key in all of these processes. It is the trigger to knowing that there is a problem. Information is needed to define and structure the problem. Information is needed to explore and choose between the alternative solutions and information is needed to evaluate the effect of the implemented choice.

Decision Making Models

In order to examine the process by which decisions are made a number of decision making models have been proposed. Three key models are rational decision making, satisficing or bounded reality, and the incremental model.

Rational Decision Making

The rational decision making model developed by economists, decision theorists and management scientists is one that is widely used and we shall return to it in Part 2. This model assumes that the decision maker has a set goal, the criteria for ranking or evaluating this goal, and a finite set of alternative potential strategies, each of which has known outcomes. The model assumes a perfect knowledge of all factors surrounding the decision and adopts a rational mechanistic approach to decision making. This is rarely possible in practice, since perfect knowledge is a rare commodity, but decision making using these assumptions is widely used. Results from rational decision making should not be used uncritically, but should, instead, be viewed as one of many types of information. Management may adjust the results of such models to an optimal decision on the basis of other factors such as uncertainty, political issues and resource issues.

Satisficing or Bounded Reality

To overcome the limitations of the rational model March and Simon proposed that individuals and organisations really search for the most satisfactory solution from the known or knowable set of solutions, rather than the optimal solution. Satisficing is a term coined by Simon to describe decision making in a complex and partially unknown environment. Satisficing proposes a descriptive, behavioural model which recognises the imperfections of knowledge and behaviour. It accepts that decision makers are not aware of all of the alternatives, and neither is there always a single clear cut objective. Decision makers may make only a limited search to discover a few satisfactory alternatives and make a decision which satisfies their aspirations, hence, the term, satisficing. Decision making can thus be described as rational, but bounded by the imperfections of the information and the decision makers' ability to perceive alternatives and outcomes. This represents a commonly adopted and practical approach to decision making. MIS can help the manager to explore a wider range of alternatives and to evaluate them more effectively by providing background information and ways of exploring the alternatives.

The Incremental Model

In this approach the decision maker does not set out any selection criteria or a set of alternatives. Instead management just muddles through. Such decision makers adopt an incremental model of decision making and select the strategy that appears only slightly different from the current mode of operation. Such an approach leads to an evolutionary sequence of small changes in an organisation's activities, such as a series of small price changes instead of one larger price change.

Decision Making Styles

Information systems must be compatible with the cognitive style of the decision maker. Cognitive style is concerned with how an individual assesses information and evaluates alternatives. Some managers are systematic and use formal procedures for gathering information about a problem and searching for the best solution. Others are more intuitive, using a wide range of information without formal search procedures. Individuals may also be classified as problem avoiders, problem seekers, and problem solvers. A manager's style is especially significant when considering the design of Decision Support Systems and Executive Support Systems.

Decision Making Environments

The environment in which the decision making takes place may influence the best approach to decision making. Key issues may be:

- Organisational structure;
- Organisational constraints.

Organisational factors may influence the speed of decision making, and the boundaries within which individuals and organisations may search for solutions.

Decision Making and Management Information Systems

MIS can perform two distinct functions with respect to decision making:

- Supply information, explore alternatives and provide support to the manager who takes the decision;

- Take the decision without the managers intervention. This is only possible with routine decisions where the decision rules are known and can be specified.

Data, Information and Decision Making

Management rarely observe operations directly. They attempt to make decisions, prepare plans and control activities by using the information that they can obtain from formal sources, such as an MIS, or informal sources, such as face to face conversations, telephone calls, social contacts, etc.

Ideally the manager should be able to define the type of information that he requires and the MIS should be able to supply it. In practice uncertainty and unpredictability mean that the process is much more ad hoc.

The manager never has access to all of the facts. Most decisions have to be based on incomplete knowledge. Either the information is not available, or it is too costly in time and money to obtain.

Nevertheless, managers need relevant information to help them to:

- plan;
- control;
- make decisions.

Relevant information is information which:

- increases knowledge;
- reduces uncertainty;
- is usable for the intended purpose.

Above we have referred to information. Some information systems managers are inclined to think that if they have provided managers with data, they have provided managers with information. But, there is a subtle difference between data and information. For example, the following definitions of data and information illustrate a commonly made distinction:

> Data are facts, events, transactions and so on which have been recorded. They are the raw materials from which information can be produced.

> Information is data that have been processed in such a way as to be useful to the recipient.

Data are facts obtained by observation, counting, measuring, weighing and like activities, which are then recorded. Much data is often concerned with the day to day transactions of the organisation. For example, the date, amount and other details of an invoice or cheque, the output for a machine, the payroll details of pay, National Insurance and tax for a person. Data may be produced as a by-product of routine operation or may require a special counting or measuring procedure. External data is often in readily usable forms, such as bank statements and purchase invoices.

Information is data that have been interpreted and understood by the recipient of the message. This process of thought and understanding means that a given message can have different meanings for different people. Also data that have been analysed, summarised or processed to produce a message or report, and described as management information only becomes information if it is understood by the recipient. The user is crucial. Information has no value in itself. Its value derives from the value of the change in decision behaviour caused by the information being available minus the cost of producing the information.

Conclusion

A Management Information System is any system that provides information to support the management activities carried out within an organisation. The three levels of management within organisations, operational, tactical and strategic, may use MIS in different ways. MIS are an important tool in management decision making. In order that MIS support decision making effectively it is important that MIS designers take into account the nature of the decision making process. There are three models of the decision making process: rational decision making, satisficing or bounded rationality, and the incremental model. Decision making styles and the environment in which decision making takes place are also important.

Managers use information in the decision making process. Information is data that have been processed in such a way as to be useful to the recipient.

Review Questions

1. What is a management information system?
2. What characterises a strategic information system?
3. What are the three elements in the strategic triangle?

4. What challenges are there for the designer of an MIS?
5. Describe the roles of strategic, tactical and operational management.
6. What do managers use information for?
7. What is a structured decision?
8. List the steps in the decision making process.
9. Distinguish between the decision making models of rational decision making and satisficing.
10. What is the difference between data and information?

2

Management Information

Objectives

When you have read this chapter you will:

- have an appreciation of the differing information requirements of different levels of management;
- appreciate the characteristics of good information;
- be aware of the range of potential information sources;
- appreciate the importance of environmental scanning to strategic management;
- be aware of the different types of information systems.

The Information Requirements of the Different Levels of Management.

In Chapter 1 the differing functions of strategic, tactical and operational management were briefly reviewed. The different levels of management are involved in decision making which is structured to a greater or lesser extent, and therefore have a range of types of information requirements. This is summarised in Figure 2.1.

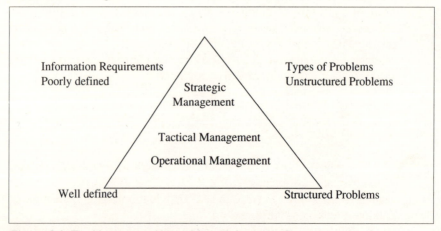

Figure 2.1: The Management Hierarchy and Information Flow.

Operational Managers:

- deal extensively with internal information;
- effective and efficient information processing is important since controls are numerous, monitoring is constant, data volumes are high and a rapid response is needed;
- internal computer based systems can handle these information requirements well;
- decisions are structured;
- optimising techniques for data analysis such as linear programming may be applicable;
- reports, action documents, such as a purchase order for materials and enquiry handling, say, to yield information such as the balance in a customer's account are central, and may be derived from internal data.

Tactical Managers:

- the span of management control is wider than at operational level, and therefore information must be drawn from a larger number of different sources;
- managers face complexity and uncertainty and require judgement, insight and good inter-personal skills;
- information is likely to be drawn from both formal and informal information systems;
- there may be no ideal information source or system;
- the environment is diverse and numerous variables must be taken into account in the decision making process, and data may be required on all of them;
- key information is concerned with the implementation of strategic objectives and the monitoring of operations;
- control systems, offering feedback are essential to support the monitoring function, and here information from budgetary, production and inventory control systems may be significant;
- managerial judgement is necessary in the identification of relevant information and its most effective application.

Strategic Managers:

- strategic management is often concerned with new and unstructured decision making situations;
- managers need to exercise flair and imagination in the collection of and interpretation of information;
- strategic information is largely external to the organisation, and key

issues are frequently competitors performance and actions, economic trends, technology changes and market changes;

- largely used to predict the future, so therefore, trends, forecasts and assessments are vital;
- qualitative as well as quantitative information is important;
- informal information sources are important;
- the information required is boundary free in the sense that it is not confined to a specific functional area or activity, and must reflect a holistic view.

This section has started to identify some of the differences between the information requirements of different levels of management, and has demonstrated that management information needs are very diverse. Any one management information system is unlikely to be able to cater for all such requirements. Managers must take some responsibility for meeting their own information requirements.

Characteristics of Good Information

As indicated by the definitions of data and information in Chapter 1, data only becomes information when it is understood by the recipient. The value of information derives from its effect on decision behaviour. If information does not lead to any decision or actions, it is valueless. When information is used to support a successful decision, the information has an intrinsic value. If information is to support effective decision making, and therefore have some value, it must possess the following characteristics:

1. Be **relevant** for its purpose, and to the problem under consideration. Relevance could be regarded as a measure of the overall usefulness of information and is in some senses a combined measure of the other characteristics of good information as indicated below. Information often needs to be presented to support a particular case. For example, sales and market research information for the Sales Manager will be different from that which is required by the organisation to give to agents, the press, the workforce and the holding company.
2. Be sufficiently **accurate** for it purpose. Absolute accuracy can not normally be achieved, and raising accuracy increases cost. Appropriate accuracy is required. Accuracy means that the data is correct. Accuracy should not be confused with precision.
3. Be as **complete** as appropriate. Again, often all information required to support a specific decision is not available, but it is essential that information be complete in respect of the key elements of the problem. In other words, it is important that all material information is available.
4. Be drawn from a source which is **reliable**. Managers must have confidence in the source. This is enhanced when:

- the source has been reliable in the past;
- there is good communication between the information producer and the manager.

Reliability implies that the information is a true indicator of the variable that it is intended to measure. This means that it has no intended bias, and that it has been collected in such a way that it is likely to be a true indicator. For example, if we were trying to gauge the size of a potential market, the information would be more reliable if a large scale, rather than a limited market research study has been conducted.

5. Information is communicated to the **right person**. Each manager has a defined sphere of activity and responsibility and should receive information to help them to execute their designated tasks. Information suppliers need to appreciate the key decision points in an organisation in order to direct information to the person who requires it.

6. Be **timely**. The urgency associated with information requirements varies between different activities. Fast response to ad hoc enquiries is essential, and the timing of regularly produced reports is also important. Reports should be produced to a time cycle that is consistent with the time cycle of the activity involved. The need for speed, especially for one-off problems can conflict with the achievement of adequate accuracy and a compromise often has to be reached.

7. Show the right **level of detail**. Too much detail confuses the issue. The level of detail should be less at higher levels of management, with a greater degree of compression and summarisation, and higher at lower levels, but should always be a little as possible. Redundant detail or noise should be avoided.

8. Communicated via an **appropriate channel** of communication. Good communication results where the sender and receive are in accord over the meaning of a particular message. Communication can take many forms. The typical output from an information system is a printed report or tabulation, and although these have their uses, it is important to remember that many managers obtain most of their information aurally.

9. Be **understandable** by the user's. The users knowledge, environmental context, the language used and user preferences all influence the success with which the message is received.

10. **Consistency**. Information must be based on homogeneous data, that is, the number and type of reporting units must be the same throughout. For example, if we were seeking to examine the total sales of all corporate stores over a period of several months, the number of stores examined should be constant, so that the data is comparable over the period of time under examination.

This list of characteristics of good information demonstrates that technical factors are only one consideration. Many of these factors are concerned with social and behavioural aspects associated with the communication of information.

Types and Sources of Strategic Information

The range of types of information as we have observed is wide, and often the managers must exercise considerable skill in identifying the best source from which to extract information.

The types of information necessary to top managers can be categorised in two different ways: according to its *function*, and according to its *content*. Figure 2.2 offers a categorisation according to the function of the information, and Figure 2.3 offers a categorisation according to the content of the information.

---

1. Comfort information - keeps managers informed about current situations or achievement levels, and allows them to know that performance is in line with expectations, e.g.
    - yesterday's sales volumes
    - this month's system down time
    - the number of customers served last week.
2. Status or progress information, which keeps managers abreast of current problems and crises, e.g.
    - status of construction work on a new manufacturing facility
    - progress on research and development effort on a new product line
3. Warning information — signals that changes are occurring, either in the form of emerging opportunities or impending troubles, e.g.
    - significant fluctuations in raw materials prices
    - results of test marketing of new products
    - difficulties in filling new posts with candidates with appropriate skills.
4. Planning information — descriptions of major future developments and programs, e.g.
    - future changes in the organisation's market
    - entry of new competitor's or product substitutes.
5. Internal Operations Information — key indicators of how the organisation or individuals are performing, which is useful for reporting the overall health of an organisation, e.g.
    - accumulated return on equity sales for the current month, quarter, and year to date, together with variance from planned sales.
6. External intelligence — information and opinions about activities in the environment of an organisation, e.g.
    - competitor and industry changes
    - financial market movements
    - political and economic fluctuations and shifts
7. Externally distributed information — information that top management need to review before its release to shareholders or distribution to the news media.

Figure 2.2: Strategic Information Classified According to Function

External Information

Markets and Competition
Demographic Trends
Economic Conditions
Industrial Structure
Social trends
Political factors
Technological change.

Internal Information

Marketing and sales information on performance, revenues, market share, distribution channels.
Production and operational information on assets, capacities, lead times, quality standards.
Financial information on profits, costs, margins, cash flows, investments
Personnel information on labour skills and availability, training, labour relations.
Research and Development Information on new products and developments.

Figure 2.3: Strategic Information Classified According to Its Subject Content

Characteristics of Strategic Information

Much of strategy making is novel and unstructured. Strategic information is often:

- largely external. Although some internal information may prove useful, much of the information required is about the environment. Typical strategic information concerns competitor's performance and actions, economic trends, technology changes, market changes and political factors.
- largely concerned with the future. Forecasts are of central concern, and must be centred on medium to longer term trends. There is less interest in data on past performance.
- qualitative as well as quantitative. Data includes opinions, judgements, insights, and observations.
- largely informal. Too structured a view stifles creativity and biases preferences towards the status quo.
- boundary free. A holistic view of the organisation must be achieved.
- multidimensional. All relevant facts must be considered, irrespective on their focus, which could be any of: personnel, production, marketing, finance, engineering or research.

Environmental Scanning

A key distinction between management information for strategic management and management information for tactical and operational managers is the need to gather information on the external environment. Strategic management is essentially associated with understanding the environment and predicting key changes, and future trends and influences on the organisation. The process by which information is gathered about the environment, whether formal or informal channels are involved, is known as environmental scanning. It is important that individual managers develop

1. *People*, including:
employees
customers
suppliers
social contacts
professional contacts.

2. *Other Organisations*, including:
Trade and commercial organisations
Local and central government departments
Banks
Other organisations acting as suppliers or customers.

3. *Published Material*, including:
Books and directories
Journals, magazines and newsletters
Local and national newspapers
Government and other reports and statistics.
Company annual reports
Stockbroker and investment reports
Market research reports
Databases
Television and associated media

4. *Events*, including:
Conferences
Seminars
Workshops
Exhibitions
Workshops
Training courses
Committees

5. *Commissioned Sources*, including:
Consultants
Market Research

Figure 2. 5: Checklist of Some Sources of Environmental Information

their own approaches to environmental scanning, if they are both to remain adequately informed, and to not be overwhelmed by the range of information available to them.

Scanning has the connotation of a rather hit and miss affair with an element of serendipity. Skilled managers develop an awareness of key sources and key indicators to watch.

A clearer picture of the nature of scanning can be garnered if we divide scanning into four different types:

1. *Undirected scanning*, where the manager explores generally with no specific purpose in mind.
2. *Conditioned scanning*, where the manager, influenced by experience or some trigger, recognises certain events or items of information, but as they are encountered in scanning rather than as a result of a specific search.
3. *Information directed scanning*, where the manager actively looks for specific information or information for a specific purpose but in an informal and unstructured fashion .
4. *Formal scanning*, where specially designed procedures or systems seek specific information or information concerning specific problems as, for example, in market research.

The essential nature of environmental information is that the list of potential information sources is endless. The strategic manager does not only need information about economic and financial factors, but must also monitor developments that are political, social, demographic, ecological and regulatory in nature. Figure 2.5 offers a short list of some typical sources.

Environmental Scanning with Electronic Information Sources

Today a number of external information sources are available in electronic form. These may be accessed either via on-line hosts or by acquiring appropriate CD-ROM databases. Figure 2.6 lists some common databases available through each of these avenues and indicates the wealth of data stored in these databases. These databases offer a myriad of different types of business, scientific, technical, legal and other information that might be invaluable in offering the manager a wider perspective of the environment in which they work, and also make it much easier to search data. To take a simple example, many newspapers are available on CD-ROM. Manual scanning of the back files of a newspaper, to say, identify any developments relating to a specific company over the past year would be a time consuming process. If the newspapers were searched on CD-ROM, the simple process of entering a company's name as a search term would retrieve all sections where the company has been cited. Similarly, a search covering developments in an industrial sector could be performed equally quickly. However, this one source may not provide the complete picture and it is usually necessary to consult a range of electronic sources.

There are many different types of databases available on CD-ROM or via on-line access to external hosts. Some databases are bibliographic, some are full text, (offering, for example, the full text of market research reports), and others offer financial and numerical data. Also the software may support the analysis of company data using a range of criteria, and may support the construction of appropriate models and the creation of graphic displays.

An important distinction between CD-ROM databases and the databases available via on-line searching of the hosts is currency. CD-ROM databases are usually only updated monthly or quarterly, so currency suffers

Database	Supplier	Contents
Lotus One Source, CD/Corporate: UK Private+	Lotus Development Corporation	130,000+ private and public UK companies. Structure information. Up to 10 years of annual financial data. Company/ industry comparison
Lotus One Source. CD/Corporate. International Public Companies	Lotus Development corporation	9,000 companies. Current financial statements. Interim reports and new items
FAME	Jordan+Sons Ltd	Financial and company data on over 125,000 UK companies
Directory of US Importers and Exporters	Dialog Information Services Inc	19,000 US exporters, 16,000 US importers - summarises export/import activity
Research Bank	ARK Info Source	Image database of international research reports covering company, industry and market information.
Keynote	ICC	Market analysis of every UK market. 220 sector reports
Financial Times	FT Profile	Newspaper. Full text. Financial information

Figure 2.6 : Some Examples of CD-ROM Databases

accordingly. On-line databases are updated more regularly, and where appropriate, may be updated in real time, or, in other words, as the data becomes available. In addition, the on-line hosts who provide access to on-line databases often offer a current awareness service from the databases which allows the manager to specify their interests in a profile and to be notified of new items, often on a weekly or monthly basis.

Information from both types of databases may be downloaded into organisational databases, subject to appropriate licensing arrangements, and provided that the organisation has appropriate text information management software and/or data analysis software can be integrated into a database that contains data derived from other sources. Alternatively, CD-ROM databases may be integrated into an organisation's information system by installing a CD-ROM drive or juke box on a distributed network. Indeed, a very important trend is the increasing integration of products, and the recognition that the searcher uses several different databases and different media.

Database	Host	Contents
Jordanwatch	Jordans	Financial and other information on over 100,000 UK companies
Moody's Company Data	Dunn + Bradstreet Corp.	Over 10,000 companies
Frost+ Sullivan	F+S Ltd	In-depth analyses and forecasts of technical and market trends. Industry specific report with 5 year forecasts.
PROMT	FT Profile Ltd	Bibliographic database covering a wide range of international business, trade and government publications.
INFOMAT	FT Profile Ltd	International database covering companies, products and industries, with a focus on Europe.
ABI/INFORM	FT Profile	US and international corporate and economic affairs
Wall Street Journal	Dow Jones	Newspaper
PHIND	DataStar	Daily on-line business information for the pharmaceutical, healthcare and agrochemical industries.
Reuters East European Briefing	Reuters	Marketing, finance, research, mergers and acquisitions.

Figure 2.7 : Some Examples of On-line Databases

Types of Information Systems

Earlier sections in this chapter have sought to emphasise the role of information in the decision making process, and have noted that information is an important asset or resource. Since information is an important asset it must be managed carefully to yield maximum benefit. Managing information is handled by the organisational information system. This information system is the combination of computers and human users that manage data collection, storage and the transformation of data into useful information. An organisation must seek to establish an information system that will meet the majority of those information needs. A common system, holding data that is available to those who need to know that data offers a number of key advantages to an organisation:

- less duplication of effort in the maintenance of databases;
- more accurate data, since the data is held in only one place it only needs to be updated once;
- better communication within the organisation since everyone that needs it has access to the same information;
- a co-ordinated approach to the information needs of the organisation.

On the other hand, information systems must be sufficiently flexible to meet the needs of users at different levels in the organisation. Facilitating the input, processing, storage, retrieval and flow of information through the organisation may require the use of several types of information system. One information system processes raw data into information for day-to-day operations, and a different one provides reports for tactical managers, and yet a different one may help strategic management to make decisions. This section briefly reviews the different types of information systems and their relationship to managerial levels in the organisation. The focus is on how these information systems work together. Further detail on most of the types of information systems described here is to be found in the chapters that follow.

All information systems are composed of the following elements:

- computer hardware — the physical equipment used in the gathering, entering and storing of data, the processing of data into information and the output of the resulting information;
- computer software — the set of programs used to operate the hardware and to process data into information;
- data stored in databases;
- procedures — the set of instructions or rules that are used to direct information system activities, for example, to instruct operators as to which system components to use, to control access to computers and outline backup activities;
- personnel — who use and operate the information system.

Transaction Processing Systems

A transaction is an event. Transaction processing systems record data about events or transactions. More explicitly transaction processing systems:

- convert raw data from operations into a machine readable form
- store transaction details;
- process transactions;
- and, if needed, print out the data.

For example if an item were sold, the transaction processing system would ensure that the sale was posted in the sales journal and later, when the invoice is raised, to the accounts receivable file, and to the inventory records. Output would be a printed list of detailed monthly statements for customers, or a screen display of items in stock.

Transaction processing systems are often dedicated to the processing of accounting, sales or inventory data.
Transaction processing systems may provide basic management information in the sense that they engage in the following operations:

- classify data — e.g. students into categories, by, say Department;
- calculate — e.g. total sales made in a period;
- sort or arrange data into sequence e.g. invoices in order according to postal code to speed distribution;
- summarisation — reduce large amounts of transaction data to a briefer form;
- storage — for later reference or for legal purposes.

Management Information Systems

Management Information Systems support managers in making decisions. They should produce meaningful reports for managerial use, for managers at all three levels. MIS are suitable for support in decision making situations where the information requirements can be determined in advance and the need for the information recurs relatively regularly. An example might be the decision to change the price of a given product. In order to make such a decision it is useful to have data on production costs, existing profitability of the product, past sales of that and other products, and the effect that a previous price rise had on sales, as well as data concerning the prices of comparable products from competitors. The data used in MIS may be drawn from many parts of the organisation. Much of the data may be collected through the transaction processing system, but other data may be collected and processed in order to support a specific decision.

Decision Support Systems

Although useful in some circumstances, the reports generated by MIS are not always appropriate. They may not provide sufficiently timely information, and they do not allow the manager to test the effect of decisions. These limitations led to the development of decision support systems (DSS). DSS are information systems that assist managers with unique, non-recurring strategic decisions, that are relatively unstructured. DSS, therefore, tend to be more prevalent at tactical and strategic levels rather than at operational levels of management. In such situations the risk of making an error is high and a mistake can have serious consequences so it is important to consider all of the alternatives and to evaluate them effectively.

In strategic decision making, a significant part of the decision problem is determining the factors to consider, or, in other words, identifying the relevant information. Some of the information needed may be in the transaction processing system, but other data may need to be collected from outside of the organisation. Examples of applications of DSS are in financial planning, police patrol analysis, and the design of a new recreation resort. DSS are often implemented on large mainframes, but personal DSS are becoming more widely used, since these offer the manager a great deal of flexibility. DSS use models, which, as a simplified version of reality, describe the interrelationships between the important variables in a particular environment, and allow the manager to explore answers to questions based on What-if?

Executive Information Systems

Executive Information Systems (EIS) are designed to assist top level executives in the acquisition and use of the information that is necessary to support them in their top management of the organisation. Top managers need to be able to achieve a quick feel for key issues, without being overloaded with detail. On the other hand quick access to detail must also be available to support the executive in the detailed investigation of a problem once the problem or opportunity has been identified. EIS focus on identifying opportunities and problem areas.

EIS may combine the power and data storage capacity of an organisational information system, with the ease of use and graphics capability of a PC. Information is transferred from the organisation's information system or from an external database to a PC. The executive then uses a mouse or similar device to select from a menu of results and presentation modes. Output on the screen is often in graphics form, or a mixture of graphics and tables. For example, a manager may wish to compare last year's sales figures with those of a competitor. In order to do this, the manager accesses reports on publicly held companies which are available from external financial databases, and then accesses the yearly sales figures for the manager's own organisation. The DSS will graphically compare the competitor's sales with the organisation's sales. A clear display with an easy to use interface is characteristic of a DSS.

Comparing MIS, DSS and EIS

MIS, DSS and EIS all support managerial decision making. It can be difficult to differentiate and to categorise systems, and a number of different approaches to categorisation can be adopted. It may be helpful to summarise the nature of these systems:

- MIS have an emphasis on report generation, and they are used primarily by lower and middle management to help them to solve well structured decisions.
- DSS have an emphasis on model building, and are used primarily by middle and upper management to assist with semi-structured and unstructured decisions.
- EIS have an emphasis on presentation and ease of use, and are primarily used by top level executives to make highly unstructured decisions based on information from a wide range of sources.

Office Information Systems

The presence of office automation systems, or office automation has had a significant impact upon the workplace. Office automation support all other information systems by providing free flow of data and information throughout the organisation, and not just within the office.

Office information systems perform different functions depending upon the nature of the office and the organisation, but typical components are:

- Text preparation, usually through word processing, but also through the use of scanners and OCR software.
- Voice and electronic mail
- Facsimile transmission, which allows a document to be instantaneously sent anywhere in the world.
- Electronic Data Interchange (EDI) which uses computers and communication links to electronically receive and transmit data. Data may include customer maps, purchase orders, invoices and associated documents.
- Electronic filing on magnetic or optical disks.
- Access to internal and external databases.
- Diaries, which indicate the location of an individual.

Typical hardware components of OIS are:

- Mainframe terminals
- PC's
- LAN cabling
- scanners
- telephones
- reproduction and fax machines

Typical software components of OIS are:

- Word processing software
- a DBMS
- LAN management software
- OCR software and
- telecommunication software

Expert Systems

Experts are valuable to an organisation, in that they possess knowledge that is key to the successful operation of the organisation. Experts are, by their very nature few in number, can be expensive and may be difficult to replace. Many organisations have developed expert systems to help to resolve the shortage of expert personnel. Expert systems usually focus on a very narrow area. They store facts and rules, known as their knowledge base, which mimic the decision making processes of a human expert. Many systems are designed to assist in situations where there is much complexity and uncertainty.

Approaches to MIS Design

Ackoff (1967) stressed some common myths governing MIS projects. The designer of an MIS should always be aware of these myths, since they still have much too wide currency. These myths can be summarised as:

- 'If only I had more information I would be able to make better decisions.' The truth is often that less, but better targeted information is what is required.
- 'The best persons to ask in order to establish what information is needed for decisions are the decision makers themselves.' Unfortunately, whilst decision makers should undoubtedly be consulted and involved, decision makers tend to offer a wide specification of information requirements in an attempt to make sure that they have covered everything and have room to change their mind. The proper starting point is an analysis of the objectives of the organisation.
- 'Management needs to be supplied with accurate, timely, relevant information for their activities and it is unnecessary for them to know how it is produced.' Although the first part of this statement is true, the second is not. Managers do need to understand the origins of the data, since this may well have significant implications for its interpretation.
- 'If information is more freely available, then departments can co-ordinate their activities more closely.' Again, this is a fallacy. More information may lead to more competition rather than more co-operation.

Having laid these fallacies to rest, we are in a stronger position to proceed to consider the approaches to the design of an MIS. The five main approaches are:

- *The by-product approach.* This was the earliest approach and is still widely encountered. In this approach the MIS is a by-product of a transaction processing system. Reports are often voluminous and poorly targeted, and are produced as a by-product of other data processing activities.

- *The null approach* is a reaction against the shortcomings of the by-product approach. It views the activities undertaken, particularly by top management as being dynamic and ever-changing. Under these circumstances, its proponents argue, the production of formal information by an MIS which reflects static requirements is inappropriate and MIS are useless. It is important to remember that the information requirements of lower management are more clearly defined and may be met by an MIS, and the advent of interactive systems with user-friendly query and report generation facilities make the production of information according to dynamically changing requirements much easier.

- *The key variable approach* assumes that certain attributes such as total cash available, profit to earning ratios of each plant, are crucial for assessing its performance, taking decisions and planning. These key variables are identified and MIS designed to provide reports on the values of these variables. Exception reporting is a variation on straight reporting. Here the value of a variable is only reported if it lies outside some predetermined normal range. Such systems tend to favour financial and accounting data at the expense of other information, but the approach does recognise that information must be selectively provided.

- *Total study processes* concentrate on establishing a comparison between the information requirements of management and the information supply of the current management information system. By extensive interviews, for example, an attempt is made to gain an overall understanding of the organisation's information needs, and identifying the failures of the current system. A Plan for filling gaps is formulated. This approach is comprehensive, but expensive of manpower and collects large amounts of data.

- *Critical success factor* approach is based on the assumption that an organisation has certain objectives and that specific factors are crucial in achieving these objectives The subsidiary goals, critical success factors and assumptions are then defined. Analysis then seeks the critical information set which is necessary to measure success in achieving these. The main value of this approach is in the design of systems for the provision of control information which is used to monitor the state of the critical success factors. The approach is information rather than data led.

In the early days of the design of MIS, it was envisaged the total system approach would be the most effective route to the design of a highly integrated MIS. The reality is that MIS tend to evolve over time. It is too complex to design the unified system as an initial project

Designing Information Systems to Support Organisational Objectives

All information systems should be designed to support organisational objectives. In most organisations this should lead to strategic information systems that change the way in which an organisation competes. Strategic Information Systems Planning or SISP, is one approach to the design of information systems which should lead to an appropriate emphasis on organisational objectives.

'A Strategic Information Systems Plan (SISP) is the process of establishing a programme for the implementation and use of information systems in such a way that it will optimise the effectiveness of the firm's information resource and use them to support the objectives of the whole enterprise as much as possible.

SISP has emerged from a realisation that earlier approaches to information systems planning which tended to be hardware and software oriented have been less successful than they might have been. Such approaches have often not produced optimum information systems. SISP involves matching computer applications with the objectives of organisation in order to maximize the return on investment in computer systems, as well as the return earned by the organisation as a whole.

Essentially, SISP emphasises that effective information systems are those that are designed to support the organisations objectives or strategies.

The products of a SISP will typically include a short term plan for the next 12 to 18 months as well as a longer term plan for the next three to five years. SISP can have a significant impact on information systems practices, resources and management, as well as on the overall performance of the organisation.

The scope of an SISP can vary considerably; sometimes it will look at the enterprise as a whole, or, alternatively may concentrate on a department or subsidiary. Time frames may vary. Sometime SISP can be used to integrate two recently merged firms or to re-structure management.

Figure 2.8 proposes twenty steps that can lead to the development of an SISP. These steps can be grouped into seven phases.

These steps demonstrate a potential methodology or approach to planning for strategic information systems. They underline the importance of designing information systems against an assessment of corporate strategy.

1. Obtain authorisation.
2. Establish a team and arrange accommodation, tools, etc.
3. Allocate responsibilities and create a timetable.
4. Determine the corporate goals, objectives, mission, etc.
5. Establish the firm's corporate strategy, explicitly or implicitly.
6. Define the Critical Success Factors.
7. Establish the Key Performance Indicators.
8. Define the critical data set.
9. Incorporate the firm's Information Technology Architecture.
10. Conduct a systems audit.
11. Rank current systems condition and prioritise current systems proposals.
12. Brainstorm for new systems and create an IT opportunities list.
13. Perform cost benefit and risk analysis.
14. Conduct filtering workshops.
15. Produce an action plan.
16. Communicate the action plan to all appropriate staff.
17. Identify and appoint project champions.
18. Arrange for top management to publicly commit to the SISP.
19. Create feedback mechanisms.
20. Update the SISP.

Figure 2.8 : Twenty steps to a SISP

1   Steps 1 - 3 are necessary to set the development of an SISP into action. First authorisation from senior management must be achieved. This authorisation should lead to the appointment of a team leader and allocation of a budget to develop the SISP.

2   Steps 4 - 8 are concerned with identifying, and if necessary formulating goals, objectives, missions and strategies, for the organisation or generally determining where the organisation is going. The process also includes identifying Critical Success Factors or factors that are key for success, and then considering Key Performance Indicators, or ways in which success can be measured. Finally, the Critical Data Set is that data which allows Key Performance Indicators to be calculated, and this needs to be defined.

3   Steps 9 - 11 consider the existing information systems through a systems audit. At the end of the systems audit there should be a clear picture of all the hardware, software and data which an organisation currently uses. The next stage is involved in evaluating the appropriateness of each of these.

4   Steps 12 - 14 identify as many information systems opportunities as possible, with the emphasis on ways in which the firm can use its information systems to obtain a competitive advantage. These opportunities are then assessed by cost benefit analysis and risk analysis. The opportunities must then be filtered in order to choose systems with superior return on investment and/or cashflows.

5   Step 15 leads to the production of an action plan. This contains a list of things to be achieved and dates for their completion
6   Steps 16 - 18 is concerned with implementation and adoption of the Action Plan.
7   Steps 19 - 20 focus on maintenance of the SISP. This involves both the creation of feedback mechanisms and the updating of the SISP.

Conclusions

The information needs of managers differ depending upon the level that they are at within the management hierarchy. In general, the information requirements of operational managers are more likely to be well defined, whilst those of strategic managers are likely to be poorly defined.

Good information must be relevant and understandable by the user. In addition other characteristics including accuracy, reliability and timeliness are important.

There are a number of different types of information used by managers. Top managers, in particular must often engage in environmental scanning in order to ensure that they are sufficiently aware of external influences.

Since information is an important asset it must be managed effectively to yield the maximum benefit for the organisation. The management of information is achieved through the organisation's information system. Information systems must be sufficiently flexible to meet the needs of users at different levels in the organisation. This has led to the development of a range of different types of information system. These include transaction processing systems, management information systems, decision support systems, executive information systems, office information systems and expert systems. There are a number of different approaches to the design of an MIS, but which ever of these is chosen the system should be planned, designed and implemented using a methodology such as Strategic Information Systems Planning, so that the information system has a strategic impact upon the organisation.

Review Questions

1.   What is the key difference between the information requirements of operational managers and those of strategic managers?
2.   'The value of information derives from its effect on decision behaviour.' Discuss.
3.   List the characteristics of good information. Are any of these characteristics less important than any others? If so, why?

4. Give some examples of the types and sources of environmental information that might be valuable for strategic managers.
5. Describe the types of environmental scanning that a manager might participate in.
6. What are the five basic components of any information system?
7. What is the relationship between transaction processing systems and management information systems?
8. How does an Executive Information System differ from a Decision Support System?
9. Why are Office Information Systems important to managers?
10. Why is the null approach to MIS design limited in its horizons?
11. Explain how Critical Success Factors can be used in the design of MIS.
12. What are the key steps in Strategic Information Systems Planning?

Case Study Questions

1. It is often argued that a manager's information requirements differ according to the level of the management hierarchy in which the individual functions. In particular, it is stated that operational managers require information in very detailed form while managers at the strategic level use summary information. Explain why this might be true in general, and consider whether it is true in an organisation known to you. Give several examples showing how the form of information changes as it moves up the hierarchy.
2. You are considering the purchase of a small pottery factory that currently manufactures a range of terracotta pots. Many of these pots are sold directly to garden centres as garden tubs, but others are sold to departmental and chain stores and some are sold in the factory shop. The total range of products includes large garden tubs, wall planters, plant pots, garlic holders, candle holders, wine coolers and tandoors. The factory is located in a small warehouse premises close to the centre of a small town. The warehouse also accommodates the factory shop. All pots are hand thrown on the premises, and the business is currently a going concern. You envisage keeping the business for three years and then selling it. Your objective is to achieve the highest possible profit in the three year period. What information do you need to decide whether the purchase is worthwhile? Is this the same information as you would use to estimate the expected profit?
3. Identify either a business or personal decision that you have made in the last six months, that you would regard as strategic i.e. it changed the way that you or your organisation was able to compete in the marketplace. Why would you describe this decision as strategic? What information did you use to help you with the decision process?
4. You are the top executive for an urban bus company operating bus services throughout Chorwell. Competition between the bus companies

in Chorwell has been aggressive and customers have been offered a range of special offers and discounts and it is increasingly difficult for the company to make a profit. One of your friends who is a local councillor passes on a rumour that one of the competing bus companies expects to cease trading in the next few weeks. This might have a significant effect on the demand for the services run by your company. How would you assess whether this information was:

  reliable;

  accurate;

  complete;

  timely?

5. One form of environmental scanning is regular reading of a newspaper. What types of information can be obtained from this source, and what are the limitations of this source? In what way would the availability of back issues on a CD-ROM improve the value of a newspaper as a source of information?

6. Review the types of information systems in use in your organisation. Identify the information systems used and categorise them according to the list that you have been given showing the types of information system.

7. Indicate whether the following situations are best support by MIS, DSS or expert systems. Why?

    (a) planning the cost feasibility of a new product with varying material and labour costs, and with likely emergence of competing products during the first year.

    (b) determining the quantity of flour for a bakery to order from suppliers each week. The quantity is determined by considering the amount of flour currently on hand and the expected demand.

    (c) diagnosing the cause of a serious medical problem that is evidenced by multiple symptoms. Diagnosis relies upon the interpretation of several different items of medical data.

    (d) determining whether to build additional holiday homes, based on the construction and operating costs, tax advantages, rental demand, and competition and position.

3

Management Information Systems

Objectives

When you have read this chapter you will:

● appreciate the relationship between transaction processing and management information systems;

● be aware of the ways in which MIS can present information to managers;

● understand the importance of DBMS and databases;

● have considered some examples of MIS.

MIS and Transaction Processing Systems (TPS)

As indicated in Chapter 2, transaction processing systems capture and operate on data related to the business of the organisation. There is an important relationship between the TPS and the MIS. Many of the data needed to support managerial decision making originate from business transactions. For example, future sales strategies must be based partly on data which shows the success of current sales promotions, policies and procedures in meeting overall marketing, profit and expense objectives. Data reflecting these issues, such as the cost of sales, the average units sold per customer, number of sales made compared to calls on customers, are captured and stored in the TPS. Without the TPS such data would not be available for summary and analysis. On the other hand, the existence of a TPS does not necessarily lead to an effective MIS. Data must be selectively used and further processed before the information needed by managers is available. In addition there are sometimes problems in integrating data from TPS and other data capture systems into a MIS. TPS, then, support MIS by providing much of the raw data.

Figure 3.1 demonstrates the relationship between a TPS and a MIS, through a Database management system, within a typical organisation. The MIS supplies information for strategic, tactical and operational decision making to all subsystems within the organisation. The information provides an essential part of the feedback mechanism in these areas and is necessary if subsystem objectives are to be achieved.

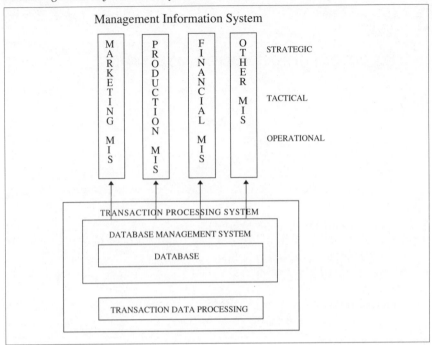

Figure 3.1: The relationship between the transaction processing system and the management information system

Figure 3.1 clearly shows the subsystems in the MIS as separate and distinct. As indicated towards the end of the first chapter, the total systems view of an MIS where the organisation establishes a global system carefully integrated into all parts of the organisation has been demonstrated to be unworkable. Such an approach tends to need to make the assumption that managers information needs can be identified or anticipated, as can ways in which information will be used, and that they are static over time. The multiple system approach recognises that there is no ideal system. The system must be developed through experience in using the system, and the addition of elements as they become necessary, understood and feasible. Changes will also be necessary to accommodate different managers, problems and activities. The MIS must draw on and integrate information from several functional area information systems, so that it is possible to provide a uniform body of knowledge. An MIS is therefore a cluster of distinct but related business systems.

Presentation of Information

The means by which MIS present data to managers is central to the effectiveness of the MIS and is likely to influence the way in which the data may be used. There are two major ways in which information can be made available to the manager:

- **Report generation**. Such reports are generally summaries of events that have taken place over a period of time, although some provide a 'snapshot' of the status of a particular resource or process at a specific time. Examples of such reports are sales or inventory reports that show the quantity of sales or the number of items in stock at a given point in time. Figure 3.2 lists the main categories of reports.

- **On-line retrieval** of information — to answer specific questions that do not require a full report. An immediate response should be available via on-line interrogation of the database.

Type of Report	Description
Regularly Scheduled	For supporting decision making — generated automatically at definite intervals and in a fixed format.
Exception	For signalling that 'out-of-bounds' conditions have arisen. Preformatted and automatically generated.
Unscheduled	For supporting decision making. Preformatted, prepared only when required by managers.
Special analysis	For supporting one-off managerial decision making. Prepared on request, based mostly on data in the organisation's files. Associated with DSS.
Inquiry Processing	For supporting decision making. A special case of the special analysis report. Users interact directly with the system and generate information through terminals. Associated with DSS.

Figure 3.2: Reports Generated from MIS

Databases and Database Management Systems (DBMSs)

Central to the provision of an effective MIS is the ability to retrieve data and use it for the production of targeted information for different purposes. Much data will be stored as the result of transaction processing operations. It is important that this data is available as a central resource for the MIS and not tied to the application that produced it. For example, sales transaction data used to update the sales ledger will be stored after the updating process. This data needs to be available for other purposes. For example, it can be used to provide reports on the performance of sales personnel, part of the personnel management function. Alternatively, it can be fed into models which use data and information from other sources to forecast cash flow and aid cash management.

The software that creates, maintains, and handles access to databases is known as a Database Management System or DBMS. The DBMS ensures that data is controlled, consistent and available. The database serves as a permanent store for the results of transaction processing, as a temporary store during processing, and as a store for the records of the transactions themselves. Interaction between the programs controlling the database is handled by the DBMS Software. This protects the database from direct contact with applications programs which carry out functions such as stock control, payroll processing and sales ledger updating. It also maintains consistency of data within the database.

A DBMS has three elements:

- definition and description software — which defines and organises data;
- processing software — which manipulates and retrieves data;
- enquiry software — which handles all requests.

Before the advent of DBMS and the database approach most TPS systems were structured by the file based approach. In the file based approach separate files were maintained for systems associated with the different functional areas. This approach led to:

- duplication of data between the different systems;
- inflexibility, since data collected for one purpose could not easily be used for another;
- concentration in design upon the system rather than the user;
- difficulties and restrictions in on-line access to files.

The database approach was developed to overcome these difficulties, and therefore has the following main attractions:

- data independence, so that data is independent of the programs which process it;
- data integrity, since data is held only once but may be used in several different processes there is no duplication of data and no opportunity for conflicting data to be held in two different parts of the system;
- flexibility, since data can be accessed in different ways for different purposes, and indeed even for new purposes that were not foreseen when the database was first compiled.

In addition, yet quite fundamentally, because all data concerning the transactions of the organisation is collected into an integrated set of files, it is much easier for management to obtain a total organisation view. The MIS can be designed relatively easily to draw on data generated by various parts of the organisation, and to prepare appropriate summary reports.

Management information systems can be subdivided to reflect specific focuses, and MIS often reflect the functional areas within an organisation. In order to understand more fully the kind of data that an MIS may generate for management and the value that they can add to an organisation it is useful to examine some of the MIS systems that support specific functional areas. We examine the major functional areas in an organisation: marketing, production and finance. Clearly the MIS relating to these areas will vary from one organisation to another but there are common characteristics. It is these characteristics that we shall attempt to summarise here. We consider MIS starting with marketing systems, and moving to production and then financial systems because this is the order in which decision making proceeds in market -led organisations.

Marketing Information Systems

A Marketing Information System is a system that covers one type of functional area. Such a system is actually a set of subsystems that interact in various ways to provide the information needed for critical decision activities. These subsystems are interrelated, share data and support the general marketing function. Also like many other MIS, the Marketing information system depends on data captured and stored during transaction processing. A typical system has the following three subsystems: sales information, product management information and marketing intelligence. Decision making should start with the market intelligence system from which
managers are able to identify customer needs . Market research should lead to product development and planning. Part of these plans is a marketing plan for the sale and distribution of the product. The product is then promoted, distributed and sold.
Typical objectives of a marketing information system are:

- management of the overall marketing process;
- direct support of sales activities and sales personnel;
- early identification of new product and service applications;
- establishment of competitive prices without sacrificing acceptable profit levels;
- control of costs related to marketing activities;
- analysis of marketing effectiveness.

For each of the main subsystems we will identify the management roles and decisions and comment on the information required.

Sales information

Management of the sales function requires the ability to close an impeding sale, to understand why past sales have occurred, to know who the customers were, and to project future sales. The sales information system will cover:

- sales analysis — the monitoring of locations of sales by sales office or geographical region. When certain regions perform above or below expectations it is important to know why.
- product analysis — the examination of sales patterns for particular products by region. When new products are introduced, valuable information may be gained by following regional performance patterns and then determining why those patterns occurred. This may mean identifying effective sales techniques, weak competition, or temporary conditions that will not be sustained.
- salesperson analysis — the determination of the differences in salesperson effectiveness. Who are the high and low achievers? why do these differences occur? Are certain sales persons better at selling certain products than others?
- sales cost analysis — the determination of the costs associated with making a sale. Estimates from sales persons expense data, and other accounting data, such as operating overheads and management support costs give an overview of costs.
- sales forecast — the prediction of futures sales, based on previous performance and other knowledge concerning the environment.

Much of the data needed in the above areas originate in the order entry and accounts receivable systems. The details captured during order processing, offer management a significant insight into customers and the performance of the sales force. Sales forecasting uses transaction data to identify evidence of evolving trends, but must also use other external indicators, such as leading economic indicators.

Product Management Information

Product management information system depend on transaction level systems such as those for inventory management, cost accounting, general ledger and cash management, and accounts payable. Within this system are applications which focus on the following features:

- pricing — the determination of the selling price of a product based on the cost to produce or acquire and market the item. This system must utilise data from the engineering or bill of materials system for costs. Item costs are also received from vendors.
- product specification — shows the features and characteristics of products. This application must also involve the bill of materials application.
- profit planning — an important aspect of a new product, planning must take into account the cost of providing a product, the potential demand, and the resulting aggregate profit that can be expected. Cost analysis data originate with the cost accounting system. Market

demand details are provided by other marketing system applications.

- financial management — this supports the organisation's management of finances in relation to the launch of new products or the maintenance of existing product lines. This system is intended to assist in planning for cash to ensure that adequate amounts are available to carry out the required tasks. Data is utilised from the general ledger and cash management systems, in conjunction with marketing planning information.
- market estimates — indications of market size or changes anticipated for a product or product line. These estimates may be stated in quantitative form or as a narrative description of evolutions expected to occur.

Not all of the data stored in this system are quantitative in nature. Qualitative information is essential for:

- New product ideas, such as requests from customers for new products and services, the identification of problems with existing products and services.
- Product evaluation including comments and suggestions from current, former or potential customers regarding the product. This is an important source of ideas for changes and modifications.
- Product planning — descriptions of development plans, including product features, a development timetable, and marketing strategies. This is often closely related to new product ideas and product evaluation. Frequently the best ideas for new products or services arise from customers. Sales calls reports and product usage information must be available within the marketing information system.

The product management information system depends on other parts of the marketing information system. For example, environmental data concerning competitors and data from the marketing intelligence system is also important.

Marketing Intelligence

Marketing intelligence systems focus on events occurring in the business environment of the organisation, such as competition and economic conditions.

Marketing intelligence systems produce the following information:

- competitors marketing strategies — descriptions and citations of the strategies used by others to market similar products.
- competitors financial profiles — which describe the financial stability of competitors and the industry as a whole. These provide information

on the capability of other firms to compete in price cutting wars, expensive advertising campaigns or research and development programmes

- product profiles — describe the strengths and weaknesses of competitors products and services, including strategies useful to sales staff for selling or marketing against other products and suggestions for substitutes attractive to customers.
- marketing research — includes details of specific product attributes, such as size, colour, packaging, brand loyalty, which has been gathered from purchased sources or original data. Such data may be general or targeted, and often includes details of product substitutes.

Ideas for promotion strategies are part of the marketing intelligence system. Thus DBEs often include details useful in promotion, such as:

- customer promotion planning — plans for advertising and sales promotion designed to penetrate a specific market or reach a certain type of customer. Estimates of costs and benefits of plans are also important.
- salesperson promotion planning — features of campaigns aimed at sales staff who market the company's product, including anticipated cost/benefit profiles and the rationale behind promotion campaigns.

Production Management Information Systems

Production management is concerned with the management of the production process. This process starts with product design and development, followed by facilities design when the production facility is modified or expanded to accommodate the new products. Continuing issues are production planning and scheduling, when the use of labour, facilities and material must be co-ordinated with the manufacture of other products. Quality control must be established and maintained and, finally the company must manage its inventory so that products are available for sale.

Again, the Production MIS comprises a number of interrelated subsystems. Data maybe derived from the TPS, other parts of the MIS, such as the Marketing MIS, and from external sources. This relationship between the different parts of the MIS within an organisation is important if the organisation is to be in a position to respond quickly to changes in its market. The Marketing MIS may signal changes in demand, and these must be communicated to managers responsible for production so that production levels can be adjusted accordingly.

Product Design

During product design, product specifications are developed, manufacturing procedures and standards are specified, materials and components to be used are determined, costs are estimated and the level of quality is specified. Product design determines the profitability of the product. Many products are designed with the aid of Computer Aided Design (CAD) systems The CAD system can significantly reduce the time that it takes for an engineer to develop a blueprint. The CAD system will also provide a bill of materials, which specifies the materials and components needed to manufacture the product. Using this information the profitability of the product can be improved via design features that improve the product, reduce costs, or enhance quality.

Facility Design

Facilities must be designed and specific operations outlined for the production of the product. Drawing packages can indicate the location of various workstations and material flows, and simulation models can help the manager to explore the best configuration. Flexible Manufacturing Systems (FMS) are systems in which workstations are flexible and can be switched from one operation to another or from one product to another with minimal set-up time. Operations are computer controlled and a product switch simply involves a program change for the workstation. These systems make it easier, quicker and cheaper to switch between products, and enhance the organisation's ability to response to shifting demand, with all of the concomitant benefits that its brings.

Production Planning and Operations

Production planning is concerned with deciding what to make, the quantities of each product that should be made, and when it should be made. This is closely related to Production operations which is concerned with ensuring that the facilities are available to manufacture the product.

Production planning draws information from a number of different sources, including the product design MIS, and the inventory control MIS and the marketing MIS. All production processes are closely linked to an organisation's purchasing and inventory TPS. Each time that a product moves from one workstation to another, materials are ordered or products are completed and sold, an entry is made in the inventory transaction system. Production planning also involves an interface with the cost accounting system to estimate the costs of producing products, and to determine the impact of productive activities on the financial plan. Typical information that is required includes:

- manufacturing specifications, product specifications and quality standards;
- the existing inventory stock of the product;
- the materials and component in stock and on order;
- a marketing plan which specifies how much product is needed;
- data indicated the personnel and equipment available for the manufacturing process.

Production operations are concerned with ensuring that appropriate resources are available to ensure that production can proceed. First it is necessary to determine if sufficient materials are available, and to consult manufacturing and product specification, and the bill of materials. These figures are then multiplied by the production run size in order to determine the total number of each part required. Manufacturing specifications also detail the manufacturing sequence, so that the schedule can determine the order in which resources are needed. Missing components must be acquired, and orders will be held up until all components are available. The production schedule will indicate for each workstation, what the operator should make, how to make them, how many to make, when to make them ad what parts to request. Production schedules must be monitored and kept up to date.

Material Requirement Planning (MRP) software can assist with the process of production scheduling It may be used to prepare the production schedule on the basis of information on what is being manufactured, new orders that require scheduling, bills of materials, issue of purchase orders for missing components, availability of personnel and facilities, ad finally customer requirements in respect of delivery timing, quality and quantity.

A more recently introduced approach to production scheduling is *Just-in-Time* (JIT). A JIT system is highly integrated, so that a product moves smoothly from one workstation to the next. Ideally in such a system, there are no excess finished goods, work in process or materials in stock. Materials, components and goods in one processing stage are not ordered until they are needed by a customer or by the next step in the process.

Quality Control

Quality control is exercised strictly in today's organisations. More effort than was previously the case has been directed towards inspecting input such as materials and enquiring the quality of labour. Coupling quality control systems with JIT or MRP systems helps to monitor production quality.

CAM and CIM

Computer Aided Manufacturing and Computer Integrated Manufacturing can have a significant effect on production scheduling.

Computer Aided Manufacturing is the use of a computer to control various aspects of the production process, including, for example, the scheduling of production activities, the monitoring of those activities and the control of individual workstations. This gives management much more control and flexibility. They can monitor each activity in the process, respond quickly to any problems , and adjust production to match changes in the market. Computers can also be used to control individual workstations via numerical control or robotics.

Computer Integrated Manufacturing is the complete integration of all of the production process steps. The entire process from design to final output is controlled by the system. Such a system enables management to enter customer requests, modify product design, change manufacturing and materials specifications, reschedule production activities, modify programs for robotics workstations, adjust quality standards and monitor the entire process.

The Production MIS has a number of facets, which may operate as separate but interrelated systems, or which in CAM and CIM are more closely integrated. The MIS always has a close relationship with the transaction processing system and the MIS covering other functional areas. An effective Production MIS is important in allowing management to change production quickly in order to respond to changes in market demand, for controlling costs, for monitoring quality and for optimising the use of resources and facilities. Throughout this section we have mentioned a number of different MIS reports. Some of the key data that must be in those reports is summarised in Figure 3.3.

Product design specifications
Manufacturing specifications
Production plan and schedule
Inventory data
Personnel data
Work orders
Cost data
Facilities and equipment data
Purchase order data for raw materials
Quality standards.

Figure 3.3: A Summary of Some of the Data Available in Production MIS

Financial Management Information Systems

Financial management have responsibility for financial planning and raising the capital to meet an organisation's objectives.. Developed from marketing and production plans, financial plans usually take the form of a budget that guides decision making. Cash must be managed to support these plans, and more cash must be obtained if the cash available is not sufficient, possibly in the form of credit. Capital acquisition decisions usually require capital budgeting. Finally the financial affairs of the organisation are audited to ensure that the financial statements represent the financial position of the organisation.

The Marketing and Production systems handle some financial data. Summary data from these sources must be available to the Financial MIS. The key subsystems in the Financial MIS are:

Financial Planning and Budgeting

A major focus for financial management are planning and budgeting activities, which integrate marketing and production plans into a financial plan. The budget process is often iterative. First a marketing plan is forwarded to management, which prepares guidelines for production, on the basis of which production prepares manufacturing plans to support the marketing plan. The budget is then forwarded to finance to ensure that the marketing and production activities can be financed.and that the budget complies with the overall strategy of the organisation. If the plans can not be financed or do not meet the general strategy, then the plans are returned for revision. Revised plans undergo the same process until all levels of management can comply with the budget.

The integration of these plans into a computer system and their availability to management either as an on-line display, or as reports, facilitates this process. It allows for ready modification of the plans, due to unforeseen events, if this is necessary.

Cash Management

A key component of the budget is the cash management plan. Cash must be enough to support activities. If cash is not sufficient then either the budget must be revised or additional funds raised. Decision support models may play a large role in the development of a cash management plan.

Funds Management

To engage in new ventures a company must raise funds or capital. The amount of necessary funds is usually determined through a series of internally generated reports. Capital may be obtained either internally, via a loan from the bank, or by issuing more stock. A plan to support a request for additional capital outlines the future revenues and expenses for the new venture.

Capital Budgeting

The management needs financial information to make capital budgeting decisions. Typical information may be the cost of the equipment, interest rates, and the cost of raising capital and other funds, the expected useful life of the equipment, operating and maintenance costs of the equipment, and the impact on cash flow of the new venture. Management must also consider this venture alongside other potential ventures, and assess the organisation's overall investment portfolio.

Auditing

There are basically two types of audit: an operational audit and a financial audit. The operational audit monitors an organisation's compliance with plans, policies and budgets. The financial audit examines the fairness of the financial statements. Operational audits are usually performed internally, and any variations reported to management for review and recommendations for appropriate changes. Internal auditors also audit the way in which information is gathered and managed. Most organisations are required to have an external financial audit. Typically the external auditor assesses the fairness of the financial statements. In both types of audits many reports emerging from the Production, Marketing and Financial MIS, together with reports from the TPS may be examined.

Financial MIS have an integrating function in drawing together financial data form other TPS and the Marketing and Production MIS. The organisation's activities can be better co-ordinated and directed towards the strategic objectives of the organisation. Figure 3.4 summarises some of the data co-ordinated and used in a Financial MIS.

Accounting data, often from the TPS
Strategic Plan
Capital market data, as in the cost of capital
Portfolio data regarding investments
Legal information on, say tax, and personnel
Marketing and production plans
Characteristics of existing Facilities
Operating and managerial policies.

Figure 3.4 : Typical Data Co-ordinated and Used in a Financial MIS

Management Information Systems and the Service Sector

The preceding sections have focused on MIS as they might be encountered in a manufacturing or production oriented environment. We have emphasised that information systems must support the strategic objectives of the organisation. Clearly different kinds of organisations have different strategic objectives. Objectives in the manufacturing sector are usually framed in terms such as the maximisation of profits, or the maximisation of market share. It is a characteristic of these objectives that they can be expressed in quantitative terms and therefore progress towards the achievement of these objectives can also be expressed quantitatively. This quantitative data can be provided by the appropriate MIS, and possibly further manipulated using a DSS. The same is not the case in the service sector.

Service Sector Organisations and their Management Information Systems

Any organisation that provides a service to its clients rather than a product can be regarded as a service sector organisation. Examples include: travel agents, hairdressers, leisure centres, libraries, airline companies, hospitals, health centres, residential care homes, social services agencies, professional practices such as lawyers and surveyors, and educational institutions. The sector is enormous.

To make the sector even larger and to cloud the issue, many organisations cannot be divided simply into manufacturing or service organisations, since they offer both services and products. This has become increasingly the case for those organisations that have used IT to achieve a competitive advantage. For example, a software house may produce a range of software products which they may sell. However, maintenance contracts, training seminars and associated support services often provide significant income for the software house, and enhance the perceived quality of the software, since appropriate support services are a relevant software evaluation criterion. The current focus throughout the public sector on quality has also led to a closer relationship between products and service.

In terms of information requirements and information systems, there are a number of significant differences between the manufacturing and service industries:

1. The establishment of performance measures is difficult. Even where such performance measures can be established it may not be possible to apply a quantitative measure. In some areas of the service sector it is easier to establish performance measures than in other areas. For instance, a major theme park may use its attendance figures as a measure of success. Hospitals, for example, may apply a combination of different measures associated perhaps with: recovery rate of patients, number of cases treated, unit cost of each treatment, occupancy of beds. Even in other parts of the health service, such as in community health, these measures may be inappropriate and other measures may need to be sought. Some of these performance measures may be difficult to

quantify, or express in such a way that it is possible to use them as a measure.

2. The service sector spans both the private and public sector and may be subject to more extensive controls and government intervention than a manufacturing organisation in the private sector. This intervention may lead to less stable strategic objectives.

3. There is unlikely to be a need for Production TPS or MIS, but other data may be maintained on the extent and nature of the use of the services offered. All organisations need management information on financial matters, and a Financial MIS should be in place in every organisation, so that top managers can readily assess the financial health of the organisation. Most organisations also need to market their services, so marketing MIS are also appropriate, but may take a quite different form from a Marketing MIS in production organisation. Marketing MIS are most likely to be comparable with the equivalent in the manufacturing sector where a service has a specified price and is sold on a one-off basis such as in the travel industry. In other sectors whether or not marketing is an appropriate activity may depend upon the cultural, social and political climate in which the organisation operates.

4. TPS are also different in the service sector, since the transactions that need to be recorded differ from those in the manufacturing sector. Some sectors, such as the travel industry and health service providers have their own specialised TPS. Since MIS often extract data from TPS, the MIS will therefore also be different in nature. For example, solicitors have case management systems showing the standard actions and events for particular case paradigms. The system then shows the progress with each case, the mount of effort (billable and otherwise) expended on each case. Other offices, such as those of accountants and insurance agents have work flow management systems covering, for instance claim handling. Since each action is tracked, it is possible to track cases, produce work lists, and oversee productivity.

In general MIS for this sector need to:

1. Offer managers a summary of the resources available for supply to customers, for example, show the number of beds in a hotel the number of classrooms in a school, the number of staff available to fulfil specified roles.

2. Offer managers a summary of how these resources are being used so that they can measure their success in the marketplace. Typical information might be: the number of books borrowed in a given month from a library, the number of operations performed, or the number of customers served.

3. Offer managers operational data on problems that have arisen, including staff problems, major queues on specified day for entrance to a leisure attraction.

4. Offer managers a summary of the financial situation, indicating how income and expenditure are adhering to budget.

The MIS may also offer access to market information, with a specific focus on any factors that are likely to trigger changes in the market position of the organisation. Relevant changes in the environment might include: changes in government legislation that may affect funding, restructuring programmes, competitors' activities, especially where there may be competition between the public and private sectors. For instance, a hospital manager will need to aware of the clinical specialisms that are offered by other hospitals in the same region, whether they be in the private or public sector. To be successful the manager must differentiate their services, either by offering a different specialism or by other factors such as quality or cost.

An Example of an MIS for the Service Sector - A Library MIS

Typically Library Management Systems maintain records of the transactions associated with the operations of a library. Typical modules are: acquisitions and ordering, cataloguing and OPAC, circulation control and serials control. Some systems also offer a dedicated management information module, but in other systems, the management information facilities are associated with the other modules, such as the acquisitions and ordering modules. Library Management Systems are well established in use, but the focus has been on the control of transactions, with limited attention to management information.

The MIS components of LMS encompass:

- facilities for handling ad hoc enquiries, for example to allow access to borrower records so that it is possible to view the details of items on loan, renewed and overdue;
- facilities for standard report generation. Figure 3.5 gives some examples of the types of reports that might be generated from the Circulation Control module of LMS;
- management information modules or report generators for the creation of ad hoc and user defined reports.

Circulation statistics
- totals
- by item
- by branch
- by category
- by borrower

Stock statistics
- items on current overdue notices
- items on hold
- items on circulation

- item activity report
- dusty stock

Borrower
- when last seen
- number of reserves
- overdues
- patron activity report
- new borrowers
- cancelled and lapsed borrowers, by borrower type.

Some systems also offer facilities for the analysis and mathematical manipulation of data, so that, for example, trends and relationships may be identified.

Figure 3.5 : Some Examples of Reports Generated by the Circulation Control Module of a Library Management System.

Conclusion

Management information systems make a wide range of different kinds of data available to managers. The MIS for an organisation is normally a series of linked subsystems covering the main functional areas. It has close links with the transaction processing system in these areas. A TPS which is designed with the use of a DBMS will offer managers more flexible access to summary information. Data in MIS is usually available to managers either in the form of a report, or via on-line retrieval.

We have reviewed the nature of, three types of MIS and the way in which they add value to the organisation: Marketing MIS, Production MIS and Financial MIS. All of these constitute a set of subsystems that interact in various ways to provide the information needed for crucial activities. Marketing MIS have subsystems covering: Sales information, Product Management Information, and Marketing Intelligence. Production MIS have subsystems covering: Product Design, Facility Design, Production Planning and Operations, and Material Requirements Planning. Financial MIS have subsystems covering Financial Planing and Budgeting, Cash Management, Funds Management, Capital Budgeting, and Auditing.

MIS for organisations in the service sector need to reflect the rather different nature of operation of these organisations. There may be difficulty in measuring strategic objectives effectively in quantitative terms. The TPS are likely to be different and sometimes specialised and since MIS are based on these, the MIS can also be expected to be different. Production MIS are unlikely to be encountered in this sector, although Marketing and Financial MIS may both have a role to play. The MIS in a Library Management System is used as an example of an MIS in the service sector.

Review Questions

1. What is the essential distinction between a TPS and an MIS?
2. List the kinds of reports generated by an MIS.
3. What are the advantages associated with the database approach to the design of a TPS as far as the user of a related MIS is concerned?
4. What are the main subsystems in a Marketing MIS?
5. Give some examples to illustrate how a Marketing MIS relies upon data generated in TPS.
6. What kind of data might be held in a Marketing Intelligence MIS? Why is this of importance to strategic managers?
7. List some of the kinds of data that are stored in a Production MIS.
8. What benefits does a Production MIS offer to an organisation?
9. Explain how Computer Integrated Manufacturing integrates the complete range of information requirements to give managers good control over the production process.
10. Why is a Materials Requirement Planning MIS necessary?
11. What are the main subsystems in the Financial MIS?
12. List the kinds of financial data that the Financial MIS might store.
13. In what sense are Financial MIS related to Marketing and Production MIS?
14. In what ways do information systems in the service sector differ from those in the manufacturing industries?
15. What are the basic functions of management information systems in the service sector?

Case Study Questions

1. A manager of a garden centre uses an information system to maintain stock control, sales records and financial control. The garden centre offers a wide range of different product lines extending from fencing and paving materials, through garden furniture such as tables and chairs, to garden pots and plants. All of the stock is seasonal, but it is particularly important to ensure that items such as annual bedding plants which are purchased from a wholesaler are sold within a few weeks of purchase. The information system has a MIS which generates the following types of reports: regularly scheduled, exception, unscheduled, special analysis, and inquiry processing. Give some examples of the type of data that might be summarised in such reports.
2. A library book supplier recently installed easy-to-use terminals in the offices of many of its customer libraries. The terminals are linked to the supplier's computer system by telephone and public data lines. Using the terminals, libraries can place orders for books, specifying the item and the quantity required. When an order is placed the system responds with price and whether the items are in stock, as well as the delivery date.

Customers like the system because it allows them to order items when they need them. For the supplier, the system provides efficient transaction processing as well as better customer service. The supplier has enjoyed an increased volume of business, partly due to this system. It can now spot trends and customer needs by analysing the data captured as a result of processing orders.

(a) What features make this system successful from the customer's viewpoint?

(b) Identify the system transactions needed to receive and process customer orders and ensure that books are available to meet their needs.

(c) Describe the relation between transaction processing and information provided to management via this system.

3. A toy manufacturer has an extensive and changing product range of quality toys. These toys are sold to large retail chains and wholesale outlets in the United Kingdom, Europe, the United States and Australia. What kind of information might the Marketing MIS provide to managers? Differentiate between information that might be available from the TPS in the organisation and information that might be collected from other sources.

4. Figure 3.5 listed some of the reports produced by a library management system. These reports are intended to offer a library manager information that may assist in the management of the library system. Explain how some of these reports might be derived from the transaction data that you would expect to encounter in the transaction processing components of a library management system.

5. A large international car manufacturer has a number of plants throughout the world. Review the kind of information that the Production MIS for one of these plants might offer to:

(a) plant management

(b) top management within the international business.

4

Decision Support Systems

Objectives
When you have read this chapter you will:
- appreciate the importance of DSS to strategic management
- be able to describe the key characteristics of DSS.
- be aware of the different types of DSS.
- be aware of the components of a DSS
- understand the role of Group DSS(GDSS)
- be aware of the implications of end-user computing.

What is a Decision Support System?

We have already introduced Decision Support Systems briefly in Chapter 2. This chapter examines DSS in more detail and in particular explores the way in which DSS may be used to support strategic decision making.

Decision Support Systems are intended to assist managers with unique strategic decisions that are semi-structured or unstructured. DSS are suited to problems where parts of the analysis can be computerised, but the decision makers' judgement and insight is needed to control the process. The computer provides support but is no substitute for the manager's judgement, and it does not provide pre-determined solutions.

DSS may be used in planning, modelling, analysing alternatives and decision making. They generally allow the user to interact with the computer systems and to use a variety of tools and procedures to develop their own systems to help in the decision making process. The emphasis is on support for decision making.

MIS are distinct from DSS in that typically the component parts of the problems that managers address are known, although the interrelationships may not be fully understood. Managers can identify the relevant factors to be studied and request information that best sheds light on them. Reports can be formulated and programs written to process the data needed for the report. Applications are handled on a recurring basis, such as daily, weekly or monthly and processing methods can be pre-specified to provide the information needed to deal with these problems and situations. MIS support structured decision making and problem solving.

In contrast a DSS deals with problems that are constantly changing, either because new sets of conditions represent one-shot, non-recurring situations or because the problem changes as the decision makers' experience broadens. In a DSS, the information to be reported is often defined by the manager at the time of need, and not in advance.

Modern DSS are usually PC's on the desks of managers with local processing power and, possibly, linked via local area networks to mainframes for easier data access. The use of spreadsheets and other modelling packages, together with DBMS combines the necessary modelling and data retrieval facilities.

Key Characteristics of DSS

The previous section has identified some of the features that characterise a DSS. Here we explore some of these characteristics in more detail.

DSS Support Semi-Structured or Unstructured Decisions

There is a large group of decisions taken by personnel in organisations that have both a structured computational and data based element as well as an unstructured or rule governed element. These decisions can be made more effectively with the use of a DSS, but the DSS does not make the decision for the decision maker.

Examples of semi-structured decisions are: planning a mix of investments in a portfolio; looking at the financial implications of the various ways of financing a short term cash flow deficit; consideration of alternative production and pricing policies; assessing the impact of potential future changes in exogenous variables, such as interest rates, analysis of the credit worthiness of corporate clients, and assessing the likely impact of departmental reorganisation.

These semi-structured decisions often also have other characteristics in common:

- they are concerned with one-off or new situations;
- the problem itself may change as more information about the problem is gathered, and new findings may shape the direction of future analysis;
- some decisions do not recur, for example, whether to pursue a merger with, or acquisition of, a particular company; but others, like preparing division budgets, financing a new sales campaign will occur more than once, but will always be semi-structured.

Data Must be Drawn form a Wide Variety of Sources

Due to the uniqueness and breadth of the issues addressed through the system, the data needed to support analyses may come from many sources. Data may come from many internal files, as well as external sources. Powerful and effective DBMS are just as important as in MIS design.

DSS are Problem Oriented

A DSS is problem oriented, in contrast to an MIS which follows the processes through an organisation. Typically DSS allow the user to asks the following kinds of questions:

What-if — allows the user to change the definition of one or more variables in a model. Typical examples might be: What is our estimated sales revenue if we achieve a 25% penetration? What would the effect on profits be if we were subject to a 3% material cost rise?

Sensitivity analysis — a special form of what-if analysis which allows the user to test whether changes from assumed variables will have a significant effect on the outcome. This is useful when a manager is uncertain of assumptions that have been made concerning a particular model variable, and they wish to asses the likely impact of any inaccuracies in these assumptions. For example, sensitivity analysis may be used to assess the sensitivity of sales to different levels of expenditure on advertising.

Goal seeking — allows users to find out the value that a particular variable must take or achieve if the desired performance level is to be achieved. For example, goal seeking might be used to find the required mix in the liquidation of short and medium term assets to reduce a projected cash deficit to zero over the next six months.

Optimisation — allows users to identify the values of a set of variables which will optimise a variable associated with outcome, such as a performance level or profit. Common forms of optimisation use linear or integer programming.

Analysis — when performance in an area of interest produces unexpected or intriguing results, the analyse function uses statistical methods to provide such data as:

- a trend line for the variables of interest over a specific period;
- the values of the variable for every period;
- the values of every variable specified.

Not all DSSs offer facilities to support the analyse function.

Simulation — Most models of business performance assume average costs and expected values for important parameters. In situations where there is a high level of uncertainty this may not be appropriate and the decision maker may wish to assess the level of risk associated with a decision. In other words they will wish to know how much they will loose if key assumptions are false. Simulation generates the information needed to assess decision risks. Through simulation, the DSS tests different combinations of variables to determine the impact on performance.

Financial functions — the financial functions consist of tools for projecting the effect of interest rates, growth patterns, and economic analysis. These are widely understood and used. Typical functions are:

- Present value calculation
- Internal rate of return determination

- Loan amortisation
- Payment calculation
- Future value determination.

DSS Involve Flexible Interactive Access to Data
DSS are designed to allow the decision maker to interact effectively with the system. This has two implications:

- the need for interactive support, so that the decision maker can ask questions or interrogate the system, using questions in the form identified above;
- the need for flexible access to data, via data retrieval and report generation facilities.

DSS are Fragmented
We have already observed that experience has shown that the totally integrated organisational MIS is unlikely to be effective. Information systems are more likely to be loose federations of subsystems, evolving separately and serving the information needs of the individual functional subsystems of the organisation. This is also the case with decision support systems, where it is even less likely that global comprehensive models can be developed for entire organisations, although, as we shall see later, a DSS framework in the form of an Institutional DSS may offer the tools for individuals to develop their own DSS to support decision making for specific problems.

DSS Development Involves End-Users
Significant onus must rest with the decision maker for the design of DSS models. The trend in modern DSS is towards end-user involvement in the development of fragmented simple models targeted to specific problems. This has become more pronounced with the increasing use of local PCs and spreadsheet modelling.

DSS are Often Developed in an IT Advanced Organisation
DSS often emerge in an organisation that already has well established IT applications for transaction processing and MIS. Such systems are often a necessary precursor to DSS, in that they both generate data that can serve as part of the input to a DSS, and also cultivate an environment in which managers view IT as a tool and are comfortable with its use. DSS are often viewed as a natural evolution in the use of information systems within an organisation, and as a stage in the movement of IT upwards in the management hierarchy.

Types of Data Processing in DSS

It is difficult to categorise DSS, and they can be categorised on the basis of a number of distinct characteristics. Here we consider DSS in relation to the types of data processing and information. There are three basic categories:

Data retrieval and analysis for decision support

These systems essentially just offer data and rely upon interaction with an existing database. Included in this group are:

- simple entry and enquiry systems, which support decisions by providing immediate interrogation of data for specific enquiries. Examples are a stock enquiry system and an airline booking system;
- data analysis systems which provide summarised and selected reports of data held on the database. For example, a system to provide information on the rate at which sales orders are being satisfied;
- accounting information systems, which are similar to data analysis systems since the accounting information is provided as an analysis of accounting transaction data. However, because accounts commonly need the same type of reports much of this information is supplied by accounting application packages.

Computational Support for Structured Decisions

These systems involve using existing general data held on a database and computation together with details of individual cases to arrive at information for a decision. Taking a motor insurance system as an example, the system accepts data on an individual, searches the database of companies terms and computes a set of calculated premiums which optimise on some group of variables such as low cost, maximum protected bonus or minimum excess.

Decision Support Involving Modelling

These systems rely on the use of existing data from a database or user input data which might be hypothetical. Using this data, consequences are calculated using a model. The model reflects relationships that the decision taker believes to hold between the variables relevant to a decision.

Types of Decision Support Systems

Decision support systems are developed using programming languages or produced by packages specifically incorporating decision support development tools. This offers an additional approach to the categorisation of DSS.

Essentially the manager needs to be able to use the mass of data in a DBMS to explore alternatives and to make decisions. To assist the manager in this process many packages are available, including packages for modelling and simulation, spreadsheets, forecasting, non-linear and linear programming, regression modelling, sensitivity and risk analysis and expert systems. We cannot discuss all of these here, but instead review the key ones.

Fourth Generation Languages

DSS may be developed using 4GL. They are useful as they are database oriented. This is important for those systems where data retrieval and analysis is key. One example of a 4GL is SQL, which can be used on many relational DBMS systems such as IBMs DB2 and ORACLE. They allow speedy application development and are end-user oriented.

Conventional high level languages such as BASIC and Pascal are not normally used to build systems, since designing DSS using these languages involves a lengthy analysis and design phase, which may well be counter productive if the decision analysis needs to be performed quickly.

Spreadsheets

Spreadsheets are the most widely used DSS. They are relatively powerful and are user friendly,such that users can build models without any specialised technical skills.Spreadsheets are most appropriate for accounting applications but also find an application for many general business modelling tasks. Some of the features that make spreadsheets useful in decision analysis are listed below:

- Spreadsheets offer a range of standard arithmetic functions, and can also calculate internal rates of return and net present value and have common statistical functions such as standard deviation.
- Individual spreadsheet models can be linked so a that figure in one may be fed into another.
- Reports are available which do not only include the worksheet or extracts from it, but also diagrams and graphs.
- Models may be developed which interact with and extract data from a database.
- What-if analysis, including optimisation and other features can be performed.
- Spreadsheets have their own high level programming language in which it is possible to write limited applications programs which interact with the spreadsheet model or which control the interaction of the spreadsheet with the user.

Spreadsheets, do, however have some limitations. Chief amongst these follow:

- Spreadsheets handle numbers best, and are poorer in handling text.
- Spreadsheet design is time consuming and must adhere to good

modelling practice. There is a tendency to produce an ad hoc model, which may be difficult to understand later.
- The basic characteristic is that the spreadsheet is based on a grid-like worksheet.

Model Generators

Model generators are traditionally, more extensive,mainframe based packages which enable speedy development of a wide range of models using interactive decision techniques. Versions are emerging that are suitable for running on more powerful microcomputers. All model generators provide model generation facilities, and incorporate many of the features of very high level languages, spreadsheet packages and statistical packages. The range of additional features offered varies, but typically includes:

- sophisticated report generation facilities;
- capacity to conduct complex statistical analysis;
- capacity to conduct time series analysis, linear programming and solutions to linear equations;
- Monte Carlo risk analysis simulations;
- sensitivity analysis;
- sophisticated financial and mathematical functions;
- consolidation of different models;
- interaction with a database.

Model generators offer complex features and are not suitable for casual end-users. This presents something of a barrier when the end-user should ideally be involved in the design of the system and the creation of models.

Institutional DSS

Institutional DSS are complete applications, designed by information systems professionals and intended to be used on a continuing basis. These systems contain a range of features to allow users to retrieve or generate information needed to address a problem area. They can be described as institutional in that they are not restricted to one area in the organisation. For example, a systems designed to support market analysis is likely to include facilities for:

- retrieval of sales and market data;
- analysis of data;
- exploration of market alternatives.

Marketing is a not a prerogative of a single department, but a function that is key to several areas of the organisation. Hence a Marketing DSS will be used by staff other than those in the Marketing Department.

DSS Tools

Just as DDS generators are used to build specific DSS, so DSS tools facilitate the creation of DSS generators. These tools include programming languages, financial and mathematical functions, optimisation, simulation and forecasting model procedures, hardware and software graphics, and database query systems. DSS tools are generally used to create the DSS generators that then create the DSS, but these tools can be used to create a specific DSS directly.

Components of a DSS

A DSS comprises three key components, although the design of these components will vary depending on the nature of the DSS. These components are:

Interface

This provides the means by which the user interacts with the system. The interface is a vehicle for entering data and building the characteristics of a model. For output the interface may include display and print features. Colour and graphics are becoming the norm.

Model Subsystem

The model subsystem manages the storage and retrieval of models and assists users in model building. However this is achieved, variables must be identified and interrelated through formulas and prescribed procedures. A database of models or the model bank, stores the models. When a user invokes a model, the model subsystem locates and retrieves it, and, with the data subsystem, loads the data for processing.

Data Subsystem

The Data subsystem includes the means for retrieval and processing of data from formal databases, and the tools to manage the data. A DSS includes two types of databases: the organisation database, and the separate DSS database, which contains summary information. Special extraction software summarises and stores the data in the DSS database. This database may contain data in different arrangements or may include unique details such as goals or targets, or unofficial, personal data. It is quicker to retrieve data from this database.

Using a DSS

The use of a DSS is an interactive process, which may be summarised by the following five steps:

1   Examine and formulate the problem so that the problem can be further studied.

2 Identify pertinent parameters and variables, to give the user an understanding of the situation.

3 Formulate the model by interrelating parameters and variables.

4 Test the model to determine the suitability of the solution by supplying data for the variables and carrying out the processing and calculation to determine the results.

5 Refine problems. The model is seldom correct the first time, and the model often needs some refinement.

Group Decision Support Systems (GDSS)

Group decision making is often encountered in business. Managers spend a high percentage of their time in meetings. Each individual in the meeting has diverse experience, points of view, varying responsibilities and information that the others do not have. There is a need to make decisions more quickly, whilst, at the same time, the business situation itself is growing more complex, and the cost of an error is higher than in the past. Exchange of information and ideas is essential and any tools that make this process more efficient will be valuable. GDSS are one such system.

Group Decision Support Systems are a type of institutional DSS, but are unique in that they support group decision making, rather than individual decision making. Such systems require well organised computer and telecommunications systems as an infrastructure.

A GDSS is designed to help groups make decisions in situations that are semi-structured. Like the individual DSS, a GDSS may be general or specialised and focused on particular topics or tasks. Key components are:

- an Interactive Computer Interface, which allows users to submit inquiries, opinions, ideas or comments;
- a Database, which is often a relational database, because, as with individual DSS, information needs can not be anticipated nor can access paths through the database be developed in advance. Flexibility in retrieval is essential;
- a Model Subsystem, to manage the storage and retrieval of models, again, as in a DSS.

Types of GDSS

GDSS can be grouped into:

1 *Decision room Systems*, where a board or meeting room is equipped with special facilities that support group decision making. A work station will be positioned by each participant and the group facilitator, and the participants will be positioned in a horseshoe formation, so that they can

see each other. A large screen will be used for the display of data, and to record ideas generated by the group, so that all participants can view data simultaneously.

2   *Linked Decision Room Systems* rely upon videoconferencing for linking decision rooms together for group decision making. Each decision room is equipped as described above. Video cameras in each of the rooms capture the discussion and transmit the discussion to other locations where images are shown on the screen. This arrangement means that all participants do not need to be in the same place, and accordingly, the need for travel is reduced.

3   *Remote Decision Network Systems* link members at a number of distinct locations through networks. Members do not require special decision rooms. Each member has access to databases and decision support software. Emerging work station and telecommunications technology allows participants to see and hear the participants on their personal display screen. Also, identical data can appear on the screen in front of all participants.

End-User Computing

The design of DSS models requires participation by decision makers. DSS are one type of system in which end-user computing is important. End-user computing has been fuelled both by the need to develop systems that speedily meet the needs of users and by the presence of easy to use software which has facilitated this process. This brief section takes the opportunity to focus on the nature and implications of end-user computing.

End-user computing describes a situation in which the intended users of an information system are involved extensively in the crafting of these systems and their applications.

The practical involvement of end-users in application development requires that they have easy access to computing facilities. Users also need:

- education and training on the use of software tools;
- assistance with the technical aspects of writing, testing and debugging applications;
- availability of reference material and documentation;
- aid in accessing and maximising the use of the organisation's databases.

These can only be provided by information systems professionals. The role of the information systems department becomes that of supporting users in their development of systems and shifts from the development of those systems.

End-user computing gives users much greater control over the design of those systems where this is appropriate. Clearly not all systems are suitable for end-user computing; for instance the main transaction processing systems which maintain the organisational database will always be developed and maintained by information systems professionals. In end-user computing the programmer and analyst intermediaries are eliminated. In addition, since systems are under the users control, the systems can be adapted as user needs change.

It is important to recognise that end-user computing can lead to a loss of control and more individuality in systems. In this context a strong information systems strategy which offers a supportive framework in which users can develop their own systems, and which has the full backing of senior management is essential. Particular risks that must be recognised and addressed are:

- Lack of centralised standards and control — specifically end-user systems may not adhere to adequate standards in respect of documentation, testing and security;
- End-user applications are likely to service local needs and objectives. For these to be generally beneficial they must congruent with organisational objectives;
- End users may produce private information systems that run counter to company policy or against the law, in respect of areas such as confidentiality and data protection.

Conclusion

Decision Support Systems are intended to assist managers with unique strategic decisions that are relatively unstructured or semi-structured. They generally allow the user to interact with computer systems and to use a variety of tools and procedures to develop their own systems to help in the decision making process.

Decision support systems can be categorised according to the type of processing that they perform. These include: data retrieval and analysis for decision support; computational support for structured decisions; and decision support involving modelling. Decision support systems can also be categorised according to hardware and software platforms. It is possible to identify fourth generation languages, spreadsheets, model generators. All DSS comprise an interface a model subsystem and a data subsystem.

Group DSS are important to support group decision making, a process that is very prevalent in organisations.

The design of DSS often involves much participation on the part of the end-user. This raises the issue of end-user computing and the role of the computing department in this process.

Review Questions

1. List three features of a DSS that characterises it as a DSS.
2. Distinguish between a DSS and an MIS.
2. What kinds of questions might be posed by a decision maker using a DSS?

3. Why are spreadsheets widely used as one tool for the development of DSS?
4. What are the key features of a model generator?
5. Explain the functions of the three components of a DSS: the interface, the model subsystem, and the data subsystem.
6. What are the steps in the use of a DSS?
7. Why are Group DSS useful within an organisation?
8. What is the difference between a Linked Decision Room System GDSS and a Remote Decision Network System GDSS?
9. How do GDSS and DSS differ, and what do they have in common?
10. What is the relationship between end-user computing and DSS?
11. What are the main hazards of end-user computing?

Case Study Questions

1. An oil company has recently acquired rights in a certain area that permit it to conduct surveys and test drilling which will lead to them lifting oil where it is found in commercially exploitable quantities. The area is considered to have good potential for finding oil in commercial quantities. Whether the tests show the possibility of ultimate success or not or even if no tests are undertaken at all the company could still pursue its drilling programme or consider selling its rights to drill in the area. What information does the manager need to decide whether to drill or to sell the rights? How might a DSS be used by the manager to analyse the alternative strategies?

2. A top manager has built a spreadsheet model which contains data about the various revenue and cost categories faced by the company. Relations are built into the system, so that, for instance, the system will change sales levels if advertising locations are increased or decreased, and show associated changes in profit levels.

   Similarly, the spreadsheet can be used to project the impact of different pay deals on the cost of manufacturing. The manager uses the spreadsheet to test the cost of different pay deals, and relates this to the level of profit for the company.

Some of the data in the spreadsheet is based in data captured during transaction processing by systems covering ordering, inventory control and production control; other values are estimated by the manager from external sources of information and input into the DSS .

(a) In what sense is this situation structured?
(b) Is a spreadsheet model of this nature recommended for this type of analysis?
    Explain.
(c) Can this system be classified as a DSS?

3. A computer-based system is used to allocate the patrol areas of police officers. By combining graphics display capabilities and access to police data, officers can view historical data about crime and public enquiries by regions of the city. By varying routes, police are able to determine whether

they can provide better protection and coverage when allocating themselves to larger areas or sections needing more attention.

What features characterise this system as a DSS?

4. Consider an organisation that manufactures and distributes lawn mowers and other small engine home and recreation vehicles. The organisation has a decentralised system of plants, warehouses and marketing regions. What types of data is the transaction processing system for such an organisation likely to store? What summary statistics might be available from such a system that might assist the following managers with decision making:

- the marketing manger of each region;
- the managers of warehouses;
- the managers of the manufacturing plants.

The top manager is concerned to achieve a more even distribution of sales of products over the year. Currently, a significant proportion of the sales are in the summer, and to allow the manufacturing plants to produce a steady output throughout the year, much stock must be stored. This is expensive and does not always lead to the stock being in optimum condition at the point of sale. How might a DSS help the top manager to investigate the strategies available to achieve this objective?

5

Executive Information Systems and Expert Systems

Objectives
When you have read this chapter you will:
- have an appreciation of the ways in which top level executives use information systems;
- understand the characteristics of an Executive Information Systems;
- be aware of the applications of Expert Systems in business;
- be familiar with the components of Expert Systems;
- be able to describe the basic characteristics of an Expert System.

Executive Information Systems

The early developers of Decision Support Systems or DSS intended that DSS would be used by top executives to support them in the decision making process. However, a major barrier became evident. In order to make DSS sufficiently powerful to solve complex problems the user needed to be knowledgeable about models and proficient in the use of the computer interface. Not many top executives took the time to acquire these skills. Middle manager and staff analysts used DSS on behalf of top managers. Top managers were short of time, and needed very easily accessible data which matched their requirements precisely.

The idea of Executive Information Systems was proposed.

A definition offered by DeLong and Rockart is:

An Executive Information System is a user friendly, graphically oriented, computer-based information system that provides rapid access to timely information and direct access to management reports.

Executive Information Systems are used directly or indirectly by executives as an investigative tool, rather than as a fixed information system. An important feature is the ability to use the data in the system to extract different pictures or views from the data. Traditionally, top managers received information from their subordinates, and to some extent an Executive Information System can eliminate the role of these subordinates and thus contribute to the flattening of the management hierarchy.

How Do Executives Use Information?

In order to understand the nature and role of an Executive Information System it is necessary to review the way in which top executives use information. This section explores activities that are common to many top level managers and relates these activities to information needs. Top executives acquire and use information for a number of reasons. Some of the most common are:

- To understand and assess situations quickly. Top level executives maintain a fast pace and often have only a few moments to spend on a particular task.
- To facilitate the business of the organisation so that the organisation runs smoothly towards its objectives. Senior managers often function more as facilitators than decision makers. Their work focuses on:
  —How to create effective organisational processes. This involves consideration of the key players in an organisation, examining how to get things into action, and related issues. In these areas interpersonal processes are key;
  —How to deal with one or two overriding concerns or very general goals. These goals may be very broad. For example, to achieve greater overall productivity, or to improve shareholder benefits.
- To confront multiple problems together. Often many problems and opportunities exist simultaneously within an organisation. The manager needs to appreciate the interrelationships and resolve a number of issues in parallel. For example, a production shortfall which limits sales levels may be the result of a conflict between manufacturing and inventory personnel over authority to determine when materials should be moved from the warehouse to the factory floor.
- To set agendas. Information assists executives in setting agendas. Top executives agendas encompass both short term e.g. 30 to 60 day agendas and exceptionally long term agendas extending to, for instance, in excess of twenty years. Agendas are also very wide, covering a broad range of financial, product, market and organisational issues. Top executives often need to develop programmes that contribute to multiple objectives, and may have vaguer goals than managers lower in the hierarchy.
- To build networks. A network is an interconnection of individuals who work in co-operation with one another to achieve an objective. Networks facilitate flow of information between network members. People networks are information and include superiors, subordinates and colleagues, as well as those outside of the organisation.
- To maintain a corporate view. Maintaining a wide view of the organisation requires appropriate information systems.
- To maintain an industry perspective. Top executives need to keep aware of developments in the environment. Information on the environment often comes from competitors, suppliers and customers.

Characteristics of Executive Information Systems

To be successful, EIS must be compatible with the management styles and responsibilities of executives. To meet the information needs of top executives an EIS must have the following features:

- Provide timely information in a form that the executive can use, and only provide needed information.
- Offer a range of presentation formats which include extensive graphics capabilities so that information is presented in an easy-to-understand form. The presentation formats should include tabular, graphic and textual data, to accommodate both personal preferences and the most appropriate display of data for any given application.
- Allow the manager to drill down to reach the information behind the graphics on the screen. This requires multiple presentation of levels of information, with each level being more detailed and focused than the preceding one. For example, if sales are low, the manager may wish to examine orders. If it transpires that there are many unfulfilled orders, the manager may examine the production schedule in order to determine whether the items for which customers are waiting are being produced. If production of the ordered items is slow, and shortage of material is a issue, it may be necessary to examine inventory and purchasing records.   .
- Allow the manager to browse, so that they can page through records of activities.
- Have a simple yet powerful interface so that learning time is minimal. Use of a mouse and direct manipulation and in some systems, touch screens is increasingly common. Graphics are widely used in the form of symbols, icons and images.
- Offer access to a wide range of internal data to support analysis of broad business issues.
- Offer access to external information, including those available from commercial data services. These services offer data on industries, companies, financial reports, stock prices and foreign exchange rates, as well as news. The main problem with these services is that they tend to provide too much detail. Providers are aware of this limitation and are starting to address the problem.
- Offer tailoring and customisation. The information needs of executives differ, and also change over time. EIS must allow tailoring of features to met these preferences, such as the design of customised reports where both the content and its display can be closely specified.
- Analytical and modelling features. Although the complexity of models was one of the reasons why top executives rejected DSS, they will use EIS to assist in answering What-if questions, if it is easy for them to do so.

Limitations of Executive Information Systems

EIS are not favoured by every top executive, and despite their advantages there remains some resistance to their use. There are two main barriers to the use of EIS which have little to do with the quality of the EIS, but arise from the environment in which the EIS is likely to be deployed. These two barriers are:

- For some managers, EIS are not compatible with their management style. The managers do not like information technology, and may, in addition, regard it as the role of a subordinate to obtain and present information;
- EIS cannot accommodate soft information, such as personal observations, opinion and narrative text based commentary. Strategic decision makers need to consider such information.

Expert Systems

Expert systems are computer systems which embody some of the experience and specialised knowledge of an expert, and thereby mimic the expert and act as a consultant in a particular knowledge area or domain. A more formal definition might be:

> An expert system is a computer-based system that uses knowledge, facts and reasoning techniques to solve problems that normally require the abilities of human experts.

Knowledge is often represented in an expert system in a knowledge base, which is a network of interconnected rules which represent the human expertise. Rules and linkages are derived from discussion with experts and analysis of their decision making behaviour.

An expert system might, for example, be designed to assist a bank manager to assess whether to grant a loan to a client. One rule in such a systems might be:

If the client is a home owner then establish:

- the amount of the mortgage
- whether there have been any payment defaults.

The system would incorporate several similar rules. The aim of the system would be to provide a recommendation, based on the bank's standard lending policy, on whether to loan to the client, the size of the loan, and any other conditions attaching to it. The system would offer decision support, rather than replace the decision because the ES would be just one of the factors that the bank manager would take into account, in making his decision.

Expert systems are, then, a type of decision support system. They are used where reasoning as distinct from computation is important in providing advice. These systems are particularly suitable for handling vague and uncertain reasoning under situations of incomplete information and data. They attempt to take into account the effects of uncertainty and judgement. This is an important characteristic of an expert.

Expert systems are part of the field known as artificial intelligence. Artificial intelligence is broadly concerned with teaching computers to accomplish tasks in a manner that can be considered intelligent.

Applications of Expert Systems

In this book our primary interest in expert systems is in their use in business decision making. Expert systems do however have a number of other uses. Early systems were in the area of medical diagnosis. In business environments, expert systems may be used for:

- training personnel;
- archiving important knowledge within an organisation;
- aiding a person in a complex procedure such as registration of a company under the Data Protection Act;
- personal tax planning;
- product pricing;
- selection of selling methods;
- credit approval in banking;
- air crew scheduling;
- designing computer systems;
- planning a large construction project;
- suggesting solutions to problems within a computer network.

The potential range of applications of expert systems in businesses increasing. It is, however, important that the domain of the Expert System is defined clearly since Expert Systems tend to be brittle at the boundaries of their area of competence.

Essentially expert systems may be utilised in any situation where human expert advice is necessary, but may be scarce or difficult to access. Examples are:

- There is a desire to reduce the cost of developing a solution to a problem, and expert advice is expensive.
- Experts are not available at the work site.
- There is a desire to develop a computer based system that uses the knowledge of the organisation's experts.

- There is a need to reach a decision that requires several human experts.
- There is a desire to retain business expertise while allowing the human expert to return to other tasks.
- There is a need to spread the cost of expertise over a large number of difficult decision making tasks.
- Expected loss (retirement) of key personnel with years of experience.

Expert Systems Components

Expert systems are designed so that the use can simply input data, answer some questions posed by the expert system, and then receive recommendations from the expert system. In order that the expert system be able to execute this interaction and offer recommendations, the expert system uses the components shown in Figure 5.1.

At the core of the expert system are the knowledge base and the inference

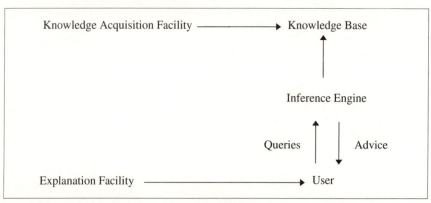

Figure 5.1   The Components of an Expert System

engine. The knowledge base includes all of the facts and rules which define the knowledge in the system. The inference engine works with these facts and rules in the knowledge base to formulate the recommendations. These components must be supported by a knowledge acquisition facility which facilitates the acquisition of knowledge from human experts, and the explanation facility, which is a part of the inference engine that can explain why or how a recommendation is reached. We will consider the role of each of these components in more detail.

The Knowledge Base

The knowledge base stores the facts and rules that represent the knowledge that has been drawn from human experts. The knowledge base can be divided into two parts:

- the domain database — this stores facts about the subject covered by the ES, and manages the facts efficiently so that they are available to the inference engine when they are needed.
- the rule database — this contains rules used in the reasoning element of the ES. Rules are stored and managed and combined with facts as needed by the inference engine. These facts and rules should include as much of an experts' experience and intuition as possible in the form of IF...THEN rules.

Inference Engine

The inference engine is the part of the system that performs the reasoning. It comprises one or more problem solving procedures. The approach used for problem solving is known as symbolic reasoning. In symbolic reasoning, symbols are used to represent the problem concepts. Various strategies and rules are applied to manipulate these symbols for decision making purposes.

The inference engine uses two basic approaches, known as backward chaining and forward chaining to arrive at a decision.

In backward chaining the inference engine seeks a path to a specific goal. An example of such a goal may be that a loan for which a customer is eligible. The inference engine assumes that the goal is true, collect all rules that support it and tests these rules to determine if they are true. If the rules are true then the original assumption is true.

In forward chaining, the inference engine start with the facts of the case. The facts are applied to the inference engine part of the rules. Rules that do not apply are eliminated until a conclusion that fits the facts is found.

The user interface is associated with the Inference Engine. The User interface includes the questions that are asked if the user and the displayed results based on the user's responses. The user interface must be easy to use.

Knowledge Acquisition Facility

If experts can formulate their knowledge in the form of rules and facts, the Knowledge Acquisition Facility provides a user friendly front end to the Knowledge base that sets up a dialogue with the expert to acquire the information.

If the expert cannot formulate knowledge in an appropriate form, or does not have the time or interest to work with the Knowledge Acquisition Facility, someone else may handle the interface on their behalf and collect the basic knowledge from the expert and input it into the system. This person is known as a knowledge engineer, and is trained in extracting rules and facts used by experts for input to an expert system. Knowledge engineers extract data from people, textbooks, databases, reports and whatever other relevant source may be available.

Explanation Facility

The Explanation Facility explains or justifies why the expert system recommends a particular decision. This justification aspect is unique to expert systems. The Explanation Facility provides the answers to *why* and *how* questions by keeping track of the rues that have been implemented in order to reach the current point in the process. For why questions, the explanation facility provides the rules being tested and the reason that the information is need to test this rule. For how questions, the explanation facility shows the line of reasoning or logic trace.

Classifying Expert Systems

Expert Systems can be classified in a number of different ways. Earlier in this chapter we have classified expert systems by their field of use. They may also be classified according to their purpose, and according to the problem area covered, e.g. interpretation, prediction, diagnosis, design, planning and monitoring. One important classification is by the type of reasoning capability of the Inference Engine.

The reasoning capabilities of the Inference engine may be either rule based or example based:

- Rule based systems are built by entering a list of IF...THEN rules. These are the more difficult to create, since every rule must be formulated in the form required by the expert system. However once built, rule based systems are more reliable since the rules have been carefully formulated directly by the exerts and system designers.
- Example based systems generate rules or conclusions from past cases or histories, which are often entered into the system as tables. The system uses inductive reasoning to create its decision making rules from these tables. The rules in an example based system depend on the quality of the examples, and may be less reliable than the rules in a rule based system, but it may be necessary to take this approach when an expert can not formulate the rules in advance in an appropriate form.

Developing Expert Systems

The first expert systems were large scale mainframe systems developed using standard languages such as FORTRAN or COBOL or artificial intelligence languages such as LISP or PROLOG. Most systems are now developed with the aid of an expert system shell. It was recognised that if the knowledge base of an existing expert system could be stripped of the facts and rules that were domain specific, a shell would be left which could be used to build other expert systems for different applications. This Shell has the mechanisms for using knowledge to make inferences, but contains no knowledge. The Shell can be used to develop an expert system. Three steps are typical:

- study the domain and collect knowledge;
- determine which expert system shell is most appropriate for the domain;
- develop the expert system by filling the shell with domain knowledge.

The approach known as prototyping is often used in the development of expert systems. Prototyping involves the development of a limited system, possibly to address a small but important part of the problem. That system is then made available to users, and tested and modified on the basis of user response. Once the first system is satisfactory, the system is extended to accommodate a further aspect of the problem. This extension is then tested and modified, and this process continues until all areas have been covered, and an expert system for the entire problem is developed.

Are knowledge based	Use large quantities of data in the form of knowledge bases to produce recommendations
Use quantitative and qualitative data	Store both quantitative and qualitative data rather than just numeric or character data associated with traditional data processing.
Uses reasoning	Uses Inference Engine to examine the details of a situation, and to draw a conclusion
Uses heuristics	Reasoning is based on the rules provided by experts who have found them helpful in dealing with certain circumstances.
Explains reasoning	Explanation facility can explain the reasoning used to formulate a specific recommendation.
Can cope with missing data	Can work around missing data to explore the impact of various alternatives.
Focus on limited subject or domain	Designed to address a very specific type of problem or situation.

Figure 5.2: Characteristics of Expert Systems

Conclusion

This chapter has briefly reviewed two types of information system that may be used by managers to assist them with decision making: Executive Information Systems and Expert Systems. Executive Information Systems are specifically designed to assist top level executives with strategic decision making and need to be carefully tailored to meet the requirements of top executives. Expert Systems are computer based systems that are designed to act as a substitute for a human expert by replicating the decision making process of an expert. After collecting information about a situation from the user, they use their accumulated knowledge of the subject to make recommendations. Both types of system represent just one tool in the decision makers' armoury. The decision maker may also need to consider other factors that are not reflected by the information system prior to making a final decision.

Review Questions

1. Why are DSS not used by top level executives?
2. Why must EIS offer access to external information?
3. Explain, using an example, the concept of drilling down.
4. Identify three ways in which the use of information by top executives differs from that of lower levels of management.
5. Distinguish between an ES and a DSS.
6. List some situations in which an ES might be used.
7. What are the main ways of classifying an ES?
8. Distinguish between a rule-based ES and an example-based ES.
9. What are the key components of an ES?
10. What is the objective of the inference engine in an ES?

Case Study Questions

1. Review the steps in the decision making process. With which of these steps can an EIS be employed?

2. The Northern Electricity Board supplies three classes of customers: residential, commercial and industrial. Residential use is highly correlated with weather because it is associated with use in heating. Commercial and industrial use is subject to variation with the general economic climate. The Board needs to be able to predict the demand and revenue for electricity for the next ten years, so that it can gauge whether is should develop its generating capacity. A top manager could use a DSS or a EIS to support them in analysing the situation. What would be the difference between the two kinds of system? Which would you recommend?

3. An engineering company that specialises in road construction would like to investigate the potential of an expert system to assist in the design of overpasses, plan the most effective routes for new roads, estimate costs, and suggest alternative bridge designs for complex intersections. Which aspects of these problems are likely to be amenable to investigation with the aid of an expert system? In what sense will this expert system capture the expertise of human experts?

4. Expert systems can be used in a wide variety of different contexts. Describe the nature of the knowledge base with if appropriate, examples for the following applications:

- training personnel in production management;
- personal tax planning;
- product pricing for new product ranges;
- credit approval in banking.

Part II

6

Models and Business Decisions

Objectives

When you have read this chapter you will:
- understand the role of model building in the decision making process;
- be aware of the basic concepts of model building that are common to any mathematical model;
- be familiar with some simple model building techniques, such as those associated with Case Models;
- be aware of the types of model building techniques available to the model builder.

The Decision Process

In Chapter 1 we defined a decision thus:

A decision is the selection of a specific course of action or solution from a set of possible alternative courses of action.

Chapter 1 listed the steps in the decision making process. It is sufficiently important that you recall these for them to be repeated here.

All decision making processes can be viewed as having eight steps:

1 Establish a single unambiguous objective against which to evaluate any outcome, and thereby define the problem. Typical examples might be: to maximise profit, to minimise costs, or to maximise quality of service.
2 State the objective in numeric or financial terms having gathered appropriate data to be able to do so.
3 Select a set of possible alternative strategies for consideration. This step can only consider those alternative strategies that are known, and therefore assumes that all alternatives are known.
4 Determine and build the model to be used to represent the strategies in terms of the objective, and identify the values (measures) of the parameters in the process.
5 Rank the alternatives.
6 Determine which strategy optimises or gives the best value for the objective established in Step 1. Choose this course of action for adoption.
7 Implement the chosen strategy
8 Monitor the success of the strategy.

You will observe that Step 4 is concerned with the determination and building of a model which is then used to evaluate the alternative strategies that are available. Model building can therefore be viewed as a central element in the decision making process. Chapter 4 also referred to models in the context of DSS. DSS use models to represent the relationships between variables and to support the exploration of alternative strategies.

Although later we will wish to consider much more complex models, the principles associated with the use of models can be illustrated with a very simple example. These principles apply however complex the model.

Example 6.1

We can sell 1000 units of a product at a price of £50 per unit. Should we accept the order?
The steps in solving this problem are:

1. Choose an appropriate objective. Here profit maximisation might be sensible.
2. Express the objective in numerical terms.
3. Identify the possible alternative strategies. Here, these are:

    *   accept the order, or
    *   reject the order.

4. Build a model to calculate the costs involved associated with both strategies. For example, say we use the following simple model which has three relationships relating a number of variables:
The first relationship calculates expense from the fixed and unit costs:

$E = a + 1000b$
    *   E is the expense
    *   a is a fixed cost of purchasing a die. Here this is known to be £5000
    *   b is the cost of producing each unit, and is known here to be £30.

The second relationship calculates the revenue:
    Revenue = Unit price x Number sold.
The third relationship calculates Profit from revenue and costs thus:
    Profit = Revenue - Costs
On the basis of this model:
the outcome of accepting the order would be a profit of
    £50,000 - £35,000 = £15000
the outcome of not accepting the order would be a profit of £0.
5. Ranking the alternatives. Accepting the order offers a profit £15000, not accepting the order offers a profit of £0.
6. Apply the profit maximisation objective established in Step 1, and choose the appropriate course of action, which here would be to accept the order.

The Basic Concepts of Model Building

The outline of the decision process above and the simple example demonstrates the central role of a model in the decision process. Such models can be constructed on a piece of paper or with the aid of a computer based system. However complex a model or the situation that it is attempting to model it is important to recognise that all models have some common factors. It is easy to forget these factors when delving into the depths of complex mathematical techniques, but they are as important to bear in mind when interpreting the results of an analysis based upon a model as achieving the correct mathematical manipulations.

Key issues to consider are:

Abstraction. All models are essentially abstractions of the real world situation. It is impossible to reflect every factor in the model, since this would lead to over complex models. The value of a model depends critically on whether the key factors in the real situation have been appropriately modelled in the model. The first stage in model building is the identification of the critical factors. Any results of the analysis based upon the model will be unreliable if the critical factors have not been appropriately identified
Simple Models. Models must be simple, so that they are:

- easy to build
- easy to understand
- easy to modify.

Sometimes it is difficult to build simple models that reflect the real world situation sufficiently well, and there is a tension between simplicity and the representativeness of the model.
Solutions
The objective of building a model is to generate some solutions which represent possible strategies. These solutions are conclusions about the behaviour of the model, and thereby of the real world situation. Decisions or actions should be based upon these solutions. A model has no real value if the decision maker does not have sufficient confidence in it to use the data that it provides in the decision making process.
Errors
Any model can be flawed. Although inexperienced model builders may introduce errors by inappropriate model building techniques, the two main sources of error are always:

- the omission of important variables or factors.
- inappropriate relationships between variables.

In order to minimise errors from these sources it is important that model builders have a good understanding of the business problem and the context in which it has arisen. There is no substitute for appropriate business knowledge.

Model building Techniques

There are many approaches to building models and although other options exist, many models are essentially mathematical in nature. Mathematics is used for model building because:

- it offers a rigorous approach, which forces the model builder to be specific about the variables and the relationships between those variables;
- powerful techniques are available for relating variables and deriving logical conclusions from given premises;
- mathematical techniques, with the aid of computers, can handle complex models.

Quantitative techniques cannot, however, be used in isolation. In Chapter 1 we emphasised that information is qualitative as well as quantitative. Qualitative information includes opinions, judgements, insights and observations. Success depends upon morale, leadership, employment, and environmental factors. A more intuitive approach is necessary to deal with these factors.

Uncertainty

Many decisions, especially strategic decisions are taken when information is imperfect and there is an element of uncertainty. This means that often the most appropriate model must accommodate this uncertainty, and this often requires recourse to probability in order to represent this uncertainty mathematically.

Example 6.1 Revisited

Suppose that the three relationships still hold but suppose that there is some uncertainty concerning the level of sales that can be achieved.It may be that there are three different levels of sales that might be achieved. Suppose that these are: 100, 250 and 1000 units respectively.
The alternative strategies remain:

- market the product, or
- do not market the product

If we decide to make each of the above numbers of units of the product the following pay off table which shows the profit depending upon the different levels of sales can be calculated, using our simple model:

Sales	Revenue	Expenses	Profit
100	5000	8000	-3000
250	12500	12500	0
1000	50000	35000	15000

Clearly provided that we can be sure to sell 1000 units we would choose to make 1000 units, but if we make 1000 units and are not sure of potential sales then we will have risked more expense than if we had only made and aimed to sell a smaller number of units.

It is clear that this is a very simple example, and not all potential strategies have been explored. We will explore additional aspects of this situation in greater depth later. For now it is sufficient to note that even this simple model can be used to investigate a decision situation where uncertainty is a factor.

Some Basic Model Building Concepts

A mathematical model is a simplification of a business situation. The simplification is achieved by including only the important elements. In a mathematical sense, models comprise two key components: variables and the relationships between those variables. The first step in model building is to select the factors or variables that the decision maker considers important. Let's look first at the variables.

Variables:

The first step in any model building process is to identify the key variables. The usefulness of a model depends crucially upon the correct identification of key variables. It can be helpful to group variables into the following categories:

Decision variables represent the main choices for the manager. They are the variables that are under the control of the decision maker. Examples are the price of a product, or the budget for advertising. The decision maker may also make other more minor decisions, such as the colour of the product, or how to brief the sales team regarding the new product. In this situation these choices are regarded as minor variables, and are not decision variables, and are therefore omitted from the model.

Exogenous variables, or external variables, are important to the problem but are not under the control of the decision maker. Typical exogenous variables are the price of raw materials, the rate of retail price inflation and the VAT rate, and the quantity that customers will buy.

Policies and constraints Policies and constraints may also be beyond the control of the decision maker, but are generally imposed by company policy or local constraints and must be recognised by the decision maker. Typical constraints may be the capacity of the plant, health and safety regulations, environmental restrictions on, say the maximum level of certain emissions that are permitted. Sometimes constraints can be modified. For example, the company may choose to expand the plant capacity. Here, then, plant capacity could be viewed as a decision variable. The dividing line between constraints and decision variables cannot be drawn too rigidly, but it is important to recognise the presence of constraints and to appreciate that they can be modified if appropriate.

Performance measures or criteria Performance measures or criteria are the quantitative expression of the objectives or goals that the decision maker is trying to achieve. Typical performance measures may be profit or market share.

Intermediate variables Some models also need to accommodate additional variables, that do not fall into any of the above categories, but which often relate to variables that do fall into the above categories. Many such variables are accounting variables that relate to cost or revenue factors, such as total revenue, and the components of manufacturing and sales costs.

Relationships:

The model or mathematical expressions which are components of the model are used to define the relationships between variables. Once these relationships have been defined it is possible to modify the value taken by one variable, and to note the effect of this change on outcomes, or the achievement of objectives. Relationships can be divided into three main types:

- *Financial relationships,* an obvious example being: Profit = Revenue - Expense.
- *Physical relationships,* expressing, for instance physical limitations, such as the amount of product that can be produced from a given quantity of raw material.
- *Judgmental relationships,* that reflect management judgement. For example the relationship between price and sales level of a product, as for example, price rises, must be based on management judgement, informed possibly by appropriate market research.Influence diagrams can be used to show which variables may be related to which others. Figure 6.1 shows a simple influence diagram. These are useful tools in the initial analysis of a situation.

Example 6.2

The model and its components described in Figure 6.1 demonstrates how a simple model may be built of a production process. First key variables are identified, and then relationships between these variables are explored and made explicit. The model can then be used to explore the effect of various strategies upon profit. Here maximisation of profit is viewed as the primary objective.

Clearly, a simple model of this kind can be handled with paper, pen and calculator, but even this model is easier to use if it is designed as a simple spreadsheet model on a computer. Under such circumstances the computer calculates the outcomes of changes in the values of specific variables, and different options can be explored very rapidly. Spreadsheets are very popular for this kind of simple model building.

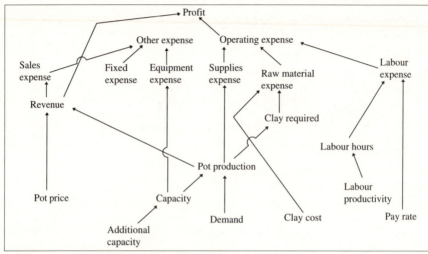

Figure 6.1: Pottery Factory-Influence Diagram

It can be difficult to envisage a model in the abstract. Hence, we introduce an example, a pottery that makes terracotta garden pots and sells these to wholesale customers such as garden centres. Although the example is based upon a real case it is somewhat simplified in order to demonstrate the elements of the model more clearly. A real world model used to support a real business decision would be more complex.

Suppose the managers of the pottery are making their plans for next year. They have two decisions to make concerning respectively manufacturing capacity and staff pay rates. The plant capacity decision involves consideration of whether the pottery should be expanded, by how much, and when. Let us suppose that if they decide to expand now, the additional capacity can be added in any quarter of next year. Expansion requires the acquisition of new equipment and additional staff. The second decision requires the management and the union to agree a pay rate for the coming year.

The company has prepared forecasts of the prices of the pots that it will sell next year as well as projections for how much could be sold. The company produces pots to order as far as possible so that no inventory of pots is held. This means that the company cannot sell more than it makes in any one period. Forecasts have also been made for the price of clay, the raw material from which the pots are made.

In order to produce pots , the company incurs expenses for labour, supplies and raw materials. Other expenses incurred relate to marketing. There are certain fixed overhead costs for each period. which also cover the costs of maintaining existing equipment.

The list of variables below summarises the key variables. This list may appear quite daunting, but it is as well to remember that this is a relatively simple model compared with real life models Although our model is simplified it is necessary to have sufficient complexity to illustrate how a model can be used.

Variables in the Pottery Model

Decision variables
PAY RATE Average hourly rate for pottery employees (£ per hour)
ADDITIONAL CAPACITY Additional pots that can be produced.
Performance Measure
PROFIT Net profit from operating the pottery each quarter (£)
Exogenous variables
POT PRICE Sales price for a pot (£)
DEMAND Demand for pots each quarter
CLAY COST Purchase cost of clay (£ per kilogram)
PRODUCTIVITY Production output (number of pots per labour hour)
Constraints and Policies
No inventory stock is maintained.
Analysis is performed quarterly.
Intermediate variables
REVENUE Revenue from sale of pots (£ per quarter)
OPERATING EXPENSE Expense associated directly with producing pots (raw material expense and labour cost per quarter)
RAW MATERIAL EXPENSE Cost of raw material (£ per quarter)
LABOUR COST Cost for labour (£ per quarter)
CLAY REQUIRED Amount of clay needed for production (kilograms per quarter)
LABOUR HOURS Amount of labour hours required for production (hours per quarter)
POT PRODUCTION Amount of pots produced (pots per quarter)
CAPACITY Actual production capacity of pottery
OTHER EXPENSE Total of other expenses, including sale expense, fixed expense and any equipment expense (£ per quarter)
SALES EXPENSE Expense for marketing pots (£ per quarter)
FIXED EXPENSE Fixed expense (£ per quarter)

Relationships

Physical Relationships
The initial capacity of the pottery is 15000 pots per quarter
    CAPACITY = INITIAL CAPACITY + ADDITIONAL CAPACITY

Remember that no inventory is held so that pot production in any quarter equals sales. If demand is higher than capacity, the company will produce to capacity. That is, production is limited by capacity. On the other hand, if demand is below capacity, then demand will limit production and sales. Thus production is limited by the smaller of capacity or demand or

POT PRODUCTION = MINIMUM (CAPACITY, DEMAND)

10 Kilograms of clay are required to make each pot. This can be expressed as:

CLAY REQUIRED = 10 x POT PRODUCTION

The total hours labour required depends on the pot production and how productive labour is, or

LABOUR HOURS = POT PRODUCTION/LABOUR PRODUCTIVITY

Financial Relationships

The remaining relationships in the model are financial. These are:

PROFIT = REVENUE - OPERATING EXPENSE - OTHER EXPENSE
REVENUE = POT PRODUCTION x POT PRICE
OPERATING COST = RAW MATERIAL EXPENSE + LABOUR EXPENSE
LABOUR EXPENSE = PAY RATE x LABOUR RATE
RAW MATERIAL EXPENSE = CLAY REQUIRED x CLAY COST

In addition, sales expense is 10 per cent of revenue, or

SALES EXPENSE = .1 x REVENUE.
Fixed expense is £10000 per quarter
FIXED EXPENSE = 10000

If the pottery acquires an additional wheel this will have production capacity of 5000 per quarter, and will incur an additional expense of £3000, together with additional staffing costs as indicated above. So we need to consider:

EQUIPMENT EXPENSE = £3000

The relationships and variables in the model have now been identified, and could, for example, be used to build a model of the business. Before we can proceed to build this model however, we need to make estimates for the exogenous variables. These estimates will be based on the manager's judgement. One function of the model will be to investigate the extent to which errors in these estimates will affect the operation of the mill. We will also need to add values for the decision variables, so that the profit can be calculated. We may then proceed to use the model to investigate different scenarios, such as different pay rates or different pottery capacities, or to investigate the effect of using different values for the exogenous variables.

Estimates for the Exogenous Variables

Variable	Unit	First Quarter	Second Quarter	Third Quarter	Fourth Quarter
Pot price	£/pot	7	7	8	8
Demand	pots	17,000	17,000	12,000	15,000
Clay cost	£/10kg	1	1	1	1.05
Labour productivity	Pots/hour	10	10	10	10

Using a Spreadsheet to Create a Model

We have now specified all of the relationships in this model and could make the calculations by hand. This would however become tedious if we wished to examine more than one case, to, for example, consider the effect of different pay rates or pot prices. This would be much more easily achieved if we were to build the model using a spreadsheet package. The precise mechanics of the construction of the spreadsheet model will vary depending upon the spreadsheet package used. However, all spreadsheets are essentially a series of cells arranged in rows and columns, into which numbers, text and formulae can be entered. Figure 6.2 shows a spreadsheet version of our model, showing the formulae which express the relationships between the variables. Figure 6.3 shows the same model, but on this occasion, the numbers are displayed. You may like to experiment with establishing this model yourself.

Once you have created a spreadsheet model it is easy to examine alternative values of the exogenous variables, and to consider, for instance the effect of changes in pay rate, clay costs or other factors.

Case Models and Scenario Analysis

If we set up the model in Figure 6.1 on a spreadsheet and then proceed to explore the effect of changing a number of different variables on the outcome, or, in other words, the effect of different strategies on the outcome, or objective, then we can explore which is the preferred strategy. Clearly, we may also explore the effect of changes in external variables, and then look at how we might most effectively modify decision variables or adopt different strategies in order to best achieve the objective.In such a situation we have built a case or scenario model. In such models the model builder considers different cases or scenarios and explores the outcome of each of these. Normally these outcomes will be compared and the strategy with the most favourable outcome will be adopted.

Figure 6.2: Pottery Base Model

	Units	First Quarter	Second Quarter	Third Quarter	Fourth Quarter	Year Total
Decision Variables						
Additional Capacity	Pots/Quarter	0	0	0	0	
Pay Rate	£/hour	5	5	5	5	
Exogenous Variables						
Pot Price	£	7	7	7.5	7.5	
Demand	Pots	17000	17000	12000	15000	
Clay Cost	£/10kg	1	1	1.05	1.05	
Productivity	Pots/hour	10	10	10	10	
Physical Factors						
Capacity	Pots/Quarter	=15000+C4	=15000+D4	=15000+E4	=15000+F4	=SUM(C14:F14)
Pot Production	Pots/Quarter	=MIN(C9,C14)	=MIN(C9,C14)	=MIN(C9,C14)	=MIN(C9,C14)	=SUM(C15:F15)
Clay Required	kg	=C15*10	=D15*10	=E15*10	=F15*10	=SUM(C16:F16)
Labour Hours Required	Hours	=C15/C11	=D15/D11	=E15/E11	=F15/F11	=SUM(C17:F17)
Financial Factors						
Revenue	£	=C15*C8	=D15*D8	=E15*E8	=F15*F8	=SUM(C20:F20)
Raw Material Expense	£	=C16*C10/10	=C16*D10/10	=C16*E10/10	=C16*F10/10	=SUM(C22:F22)
Supplies Expense	£	=5*C15/100	=5*D15/100	=5*E15/100	=5*F15/100	=SUM(C23:F23)
Labour Expense	£	=C5*C17	=D5*D17	=E5*E17	=F5*F17	=SUM(C24:F24)
Total Operating Expense	£	=C22+C23+C24	=D22+D23+D24	=E22+E23+E24	=F22+F23+F24	=SUM(C26:F26)
Sales Expense	£	=0.1*C20	=0.1*D20	=0.1*D20	=0.1*D20	=SUM(C28:F28)
Fixed Expense	£	10000	10000	10000	10000	=SUM(C29:F29)
Equipment Expense	£	=3*50	=3*50	=3*50	=3*50	=SUM(C30:F30)
Total Other Expense	£	=C28+C29+C30	=D28+D29+D30	=E28+E29+E30	=F28+F29+F30	=SUM(C32:F32)
Profit	£	=C20-C26-C32	=D20-D26-D32	=E20-E26-E32	=F20-F26-F32	=SUM(C34:F34)

Figure 6.3: Pottery Base Model

	Units	First Quarter	Second Quarter	Third Quarter	Fourth Quarter	Year Total
Decision Variables						
Additional Capacity	Pots/Quarter					
Pay Rate	£/hour	5	5	5	5	
Exogenous Variables						
Pot Price	£	7	7	7.5	7.5	
Demand		17000	17000	12000	15000	
Clay Cost	£/10kg	1	1	1	1	
Productivity	Pots/hour	10	10	10	10	
Physical Factors						
Capacity	Pots/Quarter	15,000	15,000	15,000	15,000	60,000
Pot Production	Pots/Quarter	15,000	15,000	12,000	15,000	57,000
Clay Required	kg	150,000	150,000	120,000	150,000	570,000
Labour Hours Required	Hours	1,500	1,500	1,200	1,500	5,700
Financial Factors						
Revenue	£	105,000	105,000	90,000	112,500	412,5000
Raw Material Expense	£	15,000	15,000	12,600	15,750	58,350
Supplies Expense	£	750	750	600	750	2,850
Labour Expense	£	7,500	7,500	6,000	7,500	28,500
Total Operating Expense	£	23,250	23,250	19,200	24,000	89,700
Sales Expense	£	10,500	10,500	9,000	11,250	41,250
Fixed Expense	£	10,000	10,000	10,000	10,000	40,000
Equipment Expense	£	150	150	150	150	600
Total Other Expense	£	20,650	20,650	19,150	21,400	81,850
Profit	£	61,100	61,100	51,650	67,100	240,950

There are one or two special ways in which the case or scenario analysis can be used to offer additional insight into the effect of various variables. These are:

Break even analysis, which identifies the point at which the profit is 0, i.e. gives the values of the other variables when the profit is 0.

Sensitivity or What-if Analysis which, shows what happens if this or that change is made in one of the decision or exogenous variables. By exploring the effect of changes in different exogenous variables on profit it is possible to judge how sensitive the profit is to change in specific variables, and, therefore which variables should be controlled as far as possible. This analysis is not intended to provide an optimum answer, but rather to offer an insight into the way in which key variables interrelate and the business works.

Spider diagrams, are a special kind of sensitivity analysis that can be performed for each of the exogenous variables, in order to determine the sensitivity of say, profit, to changes in each of the exogenous variables. For example, we may consider cases where each of the external variables is changed by +10% and then the cases where the change is -10%. Variables are varied one at a time, with other variables set at the base case levels (probably present levels). By trying out a series of such cases, it is possible to draw a spider diagram. The steepness of a line in a spider diagram indicates how sensitive profit is to changes in that variable. For example, the line for price might be steeper than the line for demand, so, then profit is more sensitive to changes in price than to changes in demand.

Useful insights can be developed with even these simple models, and their value should not be underestimated. Nevertheless, there are three key limitations of case models:

- they do not accommodate uncertainty
- they offer insight, but not an optimum solution
- they depend on there being a limited number of key variables, with relationships between them that can be clearly specified.

A Classification of Models and Model Building Techniques

Mathematical model building techniques deal with three different kinds of problems: simple problems, complex problems and dynamic problems. Each of these categories of model has a group of associated model building techniques. To offer a little more detail:

Simple Problems
These problems are characterised by having a small number of variables and a limited number of alternatives, and should therefore be the easiest to deal

with. The techniques for handling such problem situations are relatively straightforward and allow the exploration of the outcomes of the different strategies. Since these techniques are relatively easy to understand (you may not think so!) and apply they represent useful tools in the decision process for even the less mathematically inclined decision maker.

Two main types of techniques are applied to these problems:

(a) *Case or scenario models* where the model builder builds a simple model, and then tries out a number of cases or scenarios using different alternatives or assumptions. This method is based on trial and error. It is different from other model building approaches in that it does not use mathematical techniques to find an optimum solution. In practice, then, a solution may be identified as the best of the alternatives tested, but no procedures will have been performed to check that there is no other solution (that has not been considered) that is better.

(b) *Decision analysis models* deal with decision making under uncertainty, and make use of probability. A widely used method is decision trees.

Complex problems

Complex problems are problems where there are a large number of variables, and or many alternative strategies. It may be impossible to explore the outcome of each strategy in depth or the effect of every variable on specific outcomes. There are two main approaches:

(a) *Linear and integer programming,* which may be used to find the maximum or minimum value of an objective, subject to a set of constraints.

(b) *Simulation,* which deals with complex problems under uncertainty, using a case by case approach.

Dynamic Problems

Dynamic problems arise when it is necessary to make a series of interrelated decisions over a period of time. The outcome of the first decision may affect the options available and the outcome of subsequent decisions.

Examples of methods that might be used in this context include:

(a) *Inventory models,* which focus on economic maintenance of the correct stock levels
(b) *PERT or critical path models,* which can be particularly useful for project management.
(c) *Queuing models,* which deal with waiting or queuing situations.
(d) *Dynamic programming* which accommodates general dynamic problems.

Conclusion

All models are essentially abstractions of real world situations. To be effective models must be simple, but it is essential to identify the important variables and to specify the relationships between those variables appropriately. Business models may include the following types of variables: decision variables, exogenous variables, policies and constraints, performance measures or criteria, and intermediate variables. Relationships between variables can be divided into financial relationships, physical relationships and judgmental relationships. Case models provide a simple approach to model building that may offer the decision maker an insight into the situation. Break even analysis, sensitivity or what if analysis and spider diagrams can be useful tools in scenario analysis with Case models.

There are many mathematical model building techniques. These can be categorised in accordance with the type of problem that they seek to solve: simple problems, complex problems and dynamic problems.

Review Questions

1. Are mathematical models always an essential element in the decision making process? Give some examples of problems in which a mathematical model might assist in the decision making process. What features do these problems share?
2. What benefits accrue from simple models?
3. What are the most common sources of error in model building?
4. Why are mathematical models widely used?
5. What types of variables might you encounter in a model of a business situation?
6. When might you use case models?
7. What is sensitivity analysis?
8. What are the three main categories of model building techniques? When are dynamic models used?

Case Study Questions

A professional association publishes a journal ten times per annum. It performs all editing in-house, but printing and typesetting are performed by separate outside agencies. Editorial costs are charged on a per hour basis. Standard fees for each issue are paid to the printer and the typesetter. Paper costs and distribution costs are additional. Distribution and post and packaging costs are incurred for each copy of each issue. The journal also carries advertising, and an advertising manager is employed to attract and manage advertising. The advertising manager is paid on a commission basis according to the revenue from the advertising that they succeed in attracting. Each issue comprises 64 pages.

The print run for the journal is 23000. 20000 of these copies are distributed to members free. The remaining 3000 copies are sold to individuals and libraries. The association sells the journal for £80 per annum.

1. What are the variables in this situation? What are the relationships between the variables?
2. Build a case model, preferably on a spreadsheet which will allow you to investigate a to d:
a. If the advertising manager is successful in attracting six pages of advertising for each issue, does the journal make a profit for the association or does the association have to subsidise the journal?
b. What is the break-even point on advertising revenue i.e. how much advertising revenue must be earned in order that revenue for the journal equals its costs?
c. Assuming that the six pages of advertising is fixed, what will be the effect on the profit or loss associated with the journal of :
    (a) an increase in printing costs of £300 per issue;
    (b) a reduction in the number of editorial hours to 60 per issue.
d. Assuming the original figures, what is the break even price for the journal?

The following data should form a basis for the construction of your model:

Costs
Each issue uses 100,00 sheets of A1/A2 paper, which is then folded and cut to A5. Paper costs £10 per ream (or 200 sheets)
Editorial costs are £20 per hour. 80 hours of editorial work is required for each issue.
Printing costs are £3500 per issue
Typesetting costs are £600 per issue.
Distribution, including post and packing costs 30p per copy per issue.
Advertising manager is paid 10% of the revenue generated by the advertising.
Revenue
Subscriptions are priced at £80 each. 3000 copies are sold.
Advertising rates are £500 per page.

7

Decision Making Under Uncertainty - Pay Off Tables and Decision Criteria

---

Objectives

When you have read this chapter you will have started to explore some of the key issues associated with decision making under uncertainty. More specifically you will:

- understand the concept of a pay-off table and its use in summarising the different outcomes in an uncertain world;
- be aware that there are alternative decision rules for selecting the most appropriate strategy;
- understand the concept of dominance;
- have briefly reviewed some of the key aspects of the concepts of probability and expected value.

Revisiting the Decision Process

A key step in the decision making process is the establishment of a criterion or objective against which we might evaluate outcomes. In many of our examples we have taken profit maximisation as an appropriate decision criterion or objective, and for the sake of simplicity we will continue to use this as our objective in this section. It is important to remember that this remains our objective throughout this section, because the objective of this section is to demonstrate how much more difficult it is to ensure that a strategy is selected that will achieve this objective in a situation where uncertainty is a factor. Later we may wish to consider alternative objectives, such as achieving a specified market share, or a specified ratio between sales revenue and capital investment. The ideas presented in this section are also applicable to other objectives. In other words, whatever our objective, it becomes very much more difficult to identify the best strategy when there is uncertainty associated with the values of variables.

Before we proceed, it may be useful to ask and answer the question where does this uncertainty come from? Back in Chapter I we noted that strategic managers often deal with unstructured decision problems, where complete data is not always available and where a range of sources of information must be considered. Strategic managers are likely to face decision making under uncertainty in situations where:

1. Data on the value of certain variables is incomplete for some reason. Possibly internal data has not been collated on a particular topic, or, external data must be drawn from conflicting sources.

2. Models are being used to forecast the future. Since no one knows what will happen in the future, planning must be based on informed guesses, which carry an element of uncertainty. Simple forecasting models assume that things will continue as they always have. This is all right to give a general feel of direction, but there may be some or a great deal of uncertainty about whether things will continue as they always have.

The decision process is still then concerned with choosing the most appropriate decision strategy, but under uncertainty there are a number of possible 'states of nature' or possible events that may occur. In order to be able to handle this situation at all we have to assume that we can assign a probability to the possible occurrence of each event, so that for example, we can say how likely it is that each event may happen. These probabilities represent the uncertainty in the situation, although, often these probabilities are only guesses in their own right. The time has come to consider a simple example. This example is very simple in order to make for easier arithmetic work, and thereby to make the principles more evident:

Example 7.1

Suppose that we are selling cream buns and wish to know how many we should stock to accommodate today's sales.
Table 7.1 shows the possible levels of demand and their associated probabilities.

Table 7.1 Possible Events	
Number of buns sold (q_i)	Probability
$q_1=0$	0.05
$q_2=1$	0.60
$q_3=2$	0.35

Note: since only one of these events can occur at any one time, their respective probabilities sum to 1.

Now, we have three alternative strategies available to us:

d_1 :stock 0 buns
d_2 :stock 1 bun
d_3 :stock 2 buns

A payoff or conditional profit table can be compiled which looks at our profit in relation to each of these strategies, and considers in turn each of the possible events. Table 7.2 is such a pay-off table. The entries in the body of the pay-off table show the profit from a given strategy if a certain event occurs. A negative figure shows a potential loss, and a positive figure a potential gain. In this particular instance the pay-offs may be calculated by taking into account that buns may be:

- purchased by the retailer for 3p;
- sold to the customer for 5p;
- and that thereby the retailer makes 2p profit on each sale.

Table 7. 2: Pay-Off Table

Event: Demand is	Strategy d_1	d_2	d_3
q_1=0 buns	0	-3	-6
q_2= 1 bun	0	2	-1
q_3=2 buns	0	2	4

In order to demonstrate how the entries in this pay-off table are calculated we calculate the entry when the demand is 1 bun, and we have purchased 2 buns.
We will have paid 2 x 3p = 6p for our buns
If we sell one we achieve a revenue of 5p
Profit is then 5 - 6p = - 1p.
The compilation of a real pay off table is a major undertaking, and involves collecting data pertaining to all of the alternative strategies and evaluating each of the strategies in terms of the criterion. We introduce an additional example, Example 7.2, which demonstrates more fully the complexity associated with the compilation of a real pay-off table.

The example that is used here has been specially constructed to demonstrate the effect of applying different decision rules or criteria when it is not possible to predict what events will occur. Naturally, also, this example is simplified in that a limited number of possible events are considered. The same principles can be applied in situations where there is a spectrum of possible events but the mathematics starts to look more complex.

To return to the above pay off table, there are three possible decisions that we might take. Decision 1, the do nothing option is safe, but we shall never make any profit by doing nothing, so some risk might be appropriate. Decision 3 has more risk attached, with a larger potential loss, but a higher potential profit. Specific decision criteria have been developed to aid in the evaluation of different strategies.

Example 7.2

Suppose the potential profits and losses in millions of pounds which are expected to arise from launching various products in three market conditions can be summarised in the following pay-off table. The question is which of the three products should the company launch, if the assumption is made that they will only launch one of the three products.

Event	Decision		
	Product A	Product B	Product C
Boom Conditions	+8	-2	+16
Steady State	+1	+6	0
Recession	-10	+12	-26

And we know that the probabilities of the three market states occurring are:

Event	Probability
Boom Conditions	0.6
Steady State	0.3
Recession	0.1

Where do the figures represented in the pay-off table and the associated probabilities of the occurrence of various market states come from in a real organisation? This takes us back to Chapter 1 and 2, and demonstrates the need for strategic managers to have access to a wide variety of information sources. Figures in pay-off tables such as these are easy to produce for text book examples, but in real life they must be based on considerable quantities of data. For example, to calculate profits or losses it is essential to have an estimate of the potential revenue and costs. The calculation of costs requires that costs associated with raw materials, staffing, overheads, marketing and capital costs be considered. In order to gauge sales revenue it is necessary to judge the level of sales, and the unit price. The probability of different market states occurring must be calculated in the light of external economic indicators, data about the market conditions for this industry and this set of products, information concerning legal and socio-economic trends, and a variety of other factors.

Decision Criteria

In evaluating the alternatives in a pay-off table, managers may use one of a number of criteria. They may apply these deliberately, or inadvertently. Here we explore some of the common criteria, and briefly comment on the strengths and weaknesses of each. These criteria can also be used to evaluate the alternative strategies in decision trees, and we shall return to them in Chapter 8.

Equally Likely Criterion

This assumes that each of the potential events is equally likely. Under this assumption the possible consequences of each decision are added, and the total is divided by the total number of possible events. The strategy with the highest value is deemed to be the most desirable.

This is a sensible strategy if we have no knowledge of the relative probability of each event happening. If we do have such information, then we should use it!

If we were to apply this criterion to our example. we would choose d_2, of Example 7.1.

Maximax

When applying the maximax strategy we look for the largest possible profit that can be achieved for each strategy, and choose the strategy with the highest potential profit. Often, in practice, but not always, this strategy also has the highest possible loss associated with it. This is regarded as a go-for-it strategy, and is not prudent. Such a strategy would only be adopted by a manager who was in a position to accept high risks. In a situation where there was no uncertainty as to which event might happen, if we knew that event 3 would happen, then we would always opt for the strategy that led to the maximum profit. Uncertainty introduces risk, which means that we might choose to be more conservative.

In our example, the Maximax criterion would lead us to choose d_3 of Example 7.1.

Minimax

The Minimax criterion suggests that we choose the act with the smallest maximum possible loss, or alternatively, with the largest minimum profit. We evaluate the strategies under this criterion. Unfortunately, in practice, this criterion tends to lead to a decision to do nothing, and leads to conservation and stagnation. A decision which involves an element of risk is likely to have potential for greater success.

In our example, the application of the Minimax criterion would lead to decision d_1 of Example 7.1.

Maximum Likelihood Criterion

The Maximum Likelihood criterion leads the decision maker to choose the event that is considered to be most likely, and then to choose the best decision for that event. This approach fails to use much of the available information (i.e. that concerning the less likely events) and can therefore lead to unreasonable decisions. It is however, a criterion often used in practice by managers when they shrink from a systematic evaluation of all possible events. They start by asking themselves what is most likely to happen, and then make their decision on the basis of this predication. This can often provide a way forward when there is insufficient information, but it does offer a limited perspective.

In Example 7.1, this would lead to decision d_2 .

Expected Value Decision Criterion

Here the expected value or 'average' value of each strategy is computed, and the strategy with the highest expected value is selected. If you are not familiar with or have forgotten the concept of expected value you may find it useful to review the notes on this topic later in this chapter.

The expected value of each strategy is computed by:

- taking the probability of each event and multiplying it by the conditional profit associated with that event, and
- summing these for each strategy.

Or, mathematically,

$$\sum_{i=o}^{n} x_i p_i$$

where x_i is the conditional profit for the i th event and p_i is the probability of the i th event.

The expected value decision Rule is regarded as sensible because it uses all of the information concerning the consequences of each event, and how likely each event is to occur.

However, it does not take into account the decision makers attitude to risk. Accordingly, the criterion is most appropriate when risk is not involved in the decision, such as when the amount of money involved is small, or a decision is repetitive (e.g. as in the daily re-stocking of materials).

In practice it is often useful to calculate the expected monetary value of a set of strategies, and then to make a subjective adjustment for the risk involved in making that choice.

Example 7.1 Cont.

In our example, the expected values can be computed thus:

d_1	d_2	d_3
0x0.05=0	-3x0.05=-0.15	-6x0.05=-0.30
0x0.60=0	2x0.60=1.20	-1x0.60=-0.60
0x0.35=0	2x0.35=0.70	4x0.35=1.40

Expected Value	0	1.75	0.50

and we can see that d_2 has the highest expected value, and might therefore be selected.

Example 7.2 Contd.

In order to illustrate further the calculation of expected value we return to example 7.2. Here the expected values associated with each potential strategy can be calculated thus:

Product A = (0.6x8) + (0.3x1) + (0.1-10) = 4.1
Product B = (0.6x-2) + (0.3x6) + (0.lx12) = 1.8
Product C = (0.6x16) +(0.3x0) +(0.1x-26) = 7

This data can be entered into the pay-off table thus:

Event	Decision		
	Product A	*Product B*	*Product C*
Boom Conditions	+8	-2	+16
Steady State	+1	+6	0
Recession	-10	+12	-26
Expected Value	4.1	1.8	7

On the basis of the expected value criterion, we would select Product C as the product to market. Notice that for simplicity we have assumed that the company will only launch one product. The situation becomes much more complex if the company is prepared to consider the option of launching two products, and the market for one product may be affected by the launch of the second product. In order to consider this situation we need to examine the probabilities of the different events a little more closely.

A Summary Overview of Decision Criteria

The range of decision criteria viewed in this chapter may leave the reader with the feeling that not only do they have a decision to make, but also that they have a decision to make on how they are going to make that decision. Different decision criteria may lead to different decisions being made. What should happen from consideration of various criteria is that the decision maker will clarify their objectives, and attitudes towards risk. This insight into the mechanism of decision making and in appreciating the complexity of decision criteria is where the benefit lies. Clearly some criteria are more useful than others because they make full use of the information available. The expected value criterion is widely used, and is used in the following chapter on decision trees, but we should remember that these are averages. Actual gains or losses will be distributed about these averages.

Dominance

We have used decision criteria to choose between different courses of action. There is another factor that should also be considered when selecting between potential strategies, and that is the concept of dominance. Dominance allows for the identification of decisions that are always, in some sense, better than some other decision. There are different kinds of dominance, but dominance usually leads to the elimination of certain strategies. Dominance is usually a partial criterion in the selection of a strategy – it may be used to eliminate certain strategies, but other criteria must be applied in order to select between the remaining strategies.

For example, suppose that an organisation has to choose between different media for its advertising campaign for the following quarter. There is a choice between television, newspaper and poster advertising, there being only sufficient funds to use one medium. The actual return on the advertising outlay is measured by the estimated exposure as a result of the campaign, that is the number of potential customers who have the opportunity to see each medium. This will depend upon the weather, poor weather favouring television viewing and newspaper reading, whereas better weather gets people out of doors. Estimates of the actual exposures (in thousands of potential customers) are given for four broad but explicit descriptions of the weather, below:

Medium	**Weather**			
	Poor	*Moderate*	*Good*	*Excellent*
Television	210	190	160	120
Newspapers	190	160	150	120
Bill posters	110	140	150	200

Based upon these figures, the medium of newspaper advertising is dominated by television advertising, and therefore newspaper advertising should be eliminated from consideration.

Different Kinds of Dominance

Outcome dominance
In outcome dominance the worst profit outcome from one strategy, such as d_1 is at least as good as the best profit outcome of some other strategy, such as d_2. In other words, no matter which event takes places the dominant strategy, always leads to a more favourable outcome than the dominated strategy.

Example 7.4

Consider the following pay-off table which shows the profits from a set of potential decisions, given three possible events.

Conditional profit table

Strategy

Event	Prob	d_1	d_2	d_3	d_4
q_1	0.3	2	-1	1	1
q_2	0.2	1	0	0	0
q_3	0.5	0	-1	-1	2

Here d_1 dominates d_2, in the sense that one would never choose d_2 because d_1 would be a better option whichever event occurred.

Event Dominance
Event dominance occurs if one strategy has a profit equal to or better than that of a second strategy for each possible event. Event dominance is assessed by comparing strategies on an event by event basis.

For example, if we look at the outcomes of each event in turn, above d_1 dominates d_3 by event dominance. Also if we compare d_1 and d_2 on an event by event basis, d_1 dominates d_2 by event dominance.

Probabilistic Dominance
Probabilistic dominance is a little more complex. One act probabilistically dominates another if P(X or more) for the first is at least as large as P(X or more) for the second for all values of X. P(X or more) represents the cumulative probability of the event X.
In order to identify probabilistic dominance it is necessary to work out cumulative probabilities. To do this we start by arranging events in order in accordance with their conditional profit, say for d_1, from the lowest (-1) to the highest (2). Next we list the probability of each event adjacent to the conditional profit for the event, to produce the column P(X). We then create the values in the column P(X or more) by working from the bottom of the table and estimating the likelihood of achieving at least a given profit. So the likelihood of achieving at least 2 as profit is 0.3. Moving up to the next row, the likelihood of achieving at least 1 as profit is 0.2 +

0.3 = 0.5. We continue in this way until we have entries for all rows, and then go though the same prices's for the other strategies. The column P(X or more) shows what is referred to as the cumulative probability.

Strategy

	d_1		d_4	
Profit(X)	P(X)	P(X or more)	P(X)	P(X or more)
-1	0.0	1.0	0.0	1.0
0	0.5	1.0	0.2	1.0
1	0.2	0.5	0.3	0.8
2	0.3	0.3	0.5	0.5

Now that we have completed the table we can see that values in the column P(X or more) for d_4 are always at least as big or bigger than those for d_1. On this basis we would say that d_4 dominates d_1 by probabilistic dominance.

Some Notes About Dominance

Dominance is a useful concept but often there is no one alternative that dominates all others. Dominance can be useful in eliminating some alternatives, as we have illustrated above. We have looked briefly at three kinds of dominance, outcome dominance, event dominance and probabilistic dominance. Outcome dominance is the strongest, followed by event dominance, and then probabilistic dominance. For example, with outcome dominance one strategy very clearly offers the best option, but for probabilistic dominance it is possible for one strategy to be the best with one event and another the best with another event. Probabilitistic dominance only says that on the whole, taking all possible events into account one strategy is better than another. To think about this examine d_1 with respect to d_4.

Like decision criteria, dominance can be used in the context of decision trees, which we consider in the next chapter. It is possible to check for dominance when a decision problem has been structured in a decision tree, and thus to eliminate particular strategies. This can, in outline, be achieved by:

- examining the various strategies;
- evaluating the conditional profits and the probability of each event;
- drawing up a table showing cumulative probabilities for each profit under each strategy, as we have done above, and then identifying any dominance.

A Quick Review of Some Probability Concepts

Throughout this chapter we have used probability as a means for quantifying uncertainty in a decision making situation. We have observed that many strategic decisions involve an element of uncertainty, and therefore probability will be a recurring theme throughout this section of this book. Here we take a few moments to review some of the basic concepts concerning probability.

Objective and Subjective Probabilities

Where the probability of an event is based on past data and the circumstances are repeatable by test, the probability may be described as objective. A widely quoted example is the probability of tossing a coin and a head showing, which is 1/2 or 0.5. This value can be shown to be correct by repeated trials. If after a large number of trials we count the occurrences of heads and those of tails, we would expect a fair coin to show heads in 1/2 of the trials, and tails in the other 1/2. From this we would deduce that the probability of obtaining a head is 1/2.

Unfortunately, in most business situations it is not possible to conduct repeated trials. Here probability must be estimated on the basis of personal judgment. For example, the sales manager may feel that there is a 40% chance of obtaining an order for which their company has just quoted. Clearly this value can not be tested and has a large element of judgment and subjectivity attached to it. Different decision makers may attach different values to the probability of a specified event occurring. Nevertheless, despite the limited reliability of subjective probabilities they are often all that is available, and so they must be used in the decision making process.

Basic Rules of Probability

Whether probabilities are objective or subjective the following rules are always applicable. These rules are applicable to what are known as statistically independent events, where the occurrence of one event is completely independent of the occurrence of any other event. Below A and B are two events, and P(A) is the probability of event A occurring and P(B) is the probability of event B occurring.

1. The sum of the probabilities of all of the possible events must be 1.
2. Probabilities always lie between 0 and 1. A probability of 0 implies that the event is impossible. A probability of 1 implies that the event will happen. The smaller the probability the less likely the event.
3. Multiplication Rule (AND) and Joint Probabilities for Independent Events. This rule is used when there is a string of independent events for which the individual probability is known, and it is necessary to estimate the overall probability, or joint probability When two or more events are independent, the probability of them both occurring is equal to the product of the probabilities of the individual events. i.e.

$$P(A \text{ and } B) = P(A) \times P(B)$$

4. Addition Rule and Mutually Exclusive Events.

Two or more events are mutually exclusive if only one of the events can occur on any one trial. The probabilities of mutually exclusive events can be added to obtain the probability that one of a given collection of events will occur.

5. Conditional Probability

Conditional probability is the probability of one event happening given that another event has already occurred. For independent events, the conditional probability of the second event is the same as the probability for the remaining event, but if the events are not independent then the conditional probability will be different. The symbol used to represent conditional probability is P(A\B). P(A\B) is the conditional probability of A occurring, given that B has already occurred.

The statement concerning the conditional probability of independent events can be expressed as:

P(A\B)= P(A)

6. Marginal Probability

The marginal probability of an event is the probability of an event, if that event is not dependent on another event. Some, for example P(A) is the marginal probability of the event A. An important relationship exists between conditional, marginal and joint probabilities. This can be expressed as:

$$P(A\backslash B) = \frac{P(A \text{ and } B)}{P(B)} \qquad \text{if } P(B) \neq 0.$$

Or, in other words, the conditional probability of event A, given that event B has occurred, is equal to the joint probability of A and B, divided by the probability of event B.

This can be rewritten as:

P(A and B) = P(A\B)x P(B)

Or, the joint probability of A and B is equal to the conditional probability of A given B, times the probability of B.

A Quick Review of Expected Values

We have noted that the Expected Value Criterion is a popular criterion in the decision making process. These few notes briefly review the concept of the expected value of a random variable, and introduce some basic mathematical concepts that may be useful later.

A Random Variable is some function that assigns numerical values to each element of a set of events. The value of a random variable is one of the outcomes of a situation where there is uncertainty. In general, the value that a random variable takes is not known in advance, although the probability that the random variable will take a specific value is known in advance. By using the range of possible values that a random variable can take, together with the probability that the random variable will take a given value, it is possible to calculated the expected value of a random variable. This expected value represents a mean or average value that the random variable can be expected to take and is widely used in decision making.

To offer a more formal definition of the expected value of a random variable:

The expected value of a random variable is the sum of the values that the random variable can take, weighted by the probability that the random variable will take on that value. The expected value, is the the mean or weighted average of the values that the random variable can take.

Or $E(X) = X_i P(X_i)$

where $E(X)$ is the expected value of the random variable X
X_i is the i th value of the random variable X, and
$P(X_i)$ is the probability that X will take the value X_i.

Example 7.5 Computation of Expected Value

Values of X	Prob. of X	Weighted Probability
X=25	0.05	1.25
X=26	0.10	2.60
X=27	0.15	4.05
X=28	0.30	8.40
X=29	0.20	5.80
X=30	0.20	6.00
	E(X)=	28.10

Advantages and Disadvantages of Expected Value

Advantages
I . Summarises data effectively
2. Easy to use, understand and calculate
3. Distribution can be represented by a single figure
4. Takes account of all outcomes.

Disadvantages
I . Ignores other characteristics of the distribution, such as range and skewness
2. Assumes decision maker is risk neutral.

Some Additional Things to Note About Expected Values:

Expected Values of the Sums of Random Variables
The expected value of a sum of random variables is the sum of the expectations of those random variables, i.e.:

$$E(X + Y) = E(X) + E(Y)$$

where X and Y are two random variables

Random Variable Multiplied by a Constant
The expected value of a constant times a random variable is the constant times the expectation of the random variable:

$$E(cX) = cE(X)$$

where X is a random variable,and c is a constant

Example 7.6

In a business situation, an unknown or random variable is related to profit or cost by the following linear function:

$$P = a + bX$$

where P is profit or cost, and a and b are constants, and X is a random variable Then the expected value of profit can be expressed as:

$$E(P) = a + bE(X)$$

Now suppose that we have a situation in which monthly costs are £5000, plus £10 for each unit produced, and X is the number of units produced. Then:

$$P = 5000 + 1E(X)$$

If $E(X) = 1000$ units, then using the relationship introduced above we can calculate the value of E(P), thus:

$$
\begin{aligned}
E(P) &= 5000 + I0E(X) \\
&= 5000 + 10 \times 1000 \\
&= 15000
\end{aligned}
$$

Product of Independent Random Variables.
Suppose that we have two random variables X and Y, and these are independent. The expected value of the product XY can be expressed as the product of the expected values. That is:

$$E(XY) = E(X) \times E(Y)$$

Conclusion

Pay off tables can be used to summarise the outcomes of adopting a number of different strategies when there is some uncertainty as to which of a number of events might occur. Once a pay-off table has been constructed it is possible to evaluate each of the potential strategies by using one of a number of decision criteria. Some commonly used decision criteria are: the equally likely criterion, maximax, minimax maximum likelihood criterion and the expected value criterion. Different criteria may lead to different decisions being made. Consideration of the various criteria should help the decision maker to clarify their objectives and to gain a better understanding of the problem.

Dominance is another way to investigate alternative courses of action. Dominance allows for the identification of decisions that are in some sense better than some other decision. There are three different kinds of dominance: outcome dominance, event dominance and probabilistic dominance.

The chapter concludes with a brief review of expected values and probability; both concepts are important in decision making and we shall encounter them again in subsequent chapters.

Review Questions

1. Why is decision making often conducted under uncertainty'?
2. What does a pay-off table show?
3. List the common decision making criteria.
4. Which decision making criteria make use of the information available on the probability of occurrence of possible events?
5. When is it sensible to use the equally likely criterion?
6. What is the difference between outcome dominance and event dominance?
7. What are the advantages and disadvantages of expected value?
8. What is the difference between objective and subjective probability?
9. Distinguish between conditional and marginal probability.

Case Study Questions

Decision Criteria
1. Consider the strategies, the profits for which are shown in the accompanying table. Indicate which strategy or strategies is best under the following criteria:

a. equally likely events
b. minimax

c. maximum likelihood
d. expected value

Event	Probability	Strategy					
		d_1	d_2	d_3	d_4	d_5	d_6
q_1	.2	0	0	-4	5	-1	5
q_2	.2	0	5	-4	0	2	5
q_3	.4	0	2	3	3	5	0
q_4	.2	0	-3	6	6	3	5

e. Which of the above strategies are involved in outcome dominance?
f. Which strategies are involved in event dominance?
g. Which strategies are involved in probabilistic dominance?
h. Which strategies are undominated by any form of dominance?
2. Consider the case model that was constructed in the previous chapter. How might this be used to develop a pay-off table that will assist the manager to evaluate the available strategies?
3. Consider some business decision with which you are familiar. Identify the strategies and events, and make rough estimates of the conditional profits. What criteria do you think should be used to make the decision? Consider the relative merits of assuming equally likely events, minimax, maximum likelihood, dominance and expected value decision rules. Which criteria would you use?
4. A company has the opportunity to purchase one of three different sites for the development of its new out-of-town store. The table below shows the three possible sites with likely payoffs and associated probabilities. Construct a pay off table and then:

(a) Using the criterion of dominance, compare the alternatives. Can you find a preferred alternative? What form of dominance did you use to select your choice?
(b) Using the expected value criterion, what choice would you make?

Probabilities for Payoffs Associated With Each Site

Payoff	Investment A	Investment B	Investment C
-50	0.4	0.2	0.2
0	0.0	0.0	0.1
50	0.4	0.2	0.1
100	0.2	0.4	0.6
150	0.0	0.2	0.0

5. A frozen food company has three options for agreeing the price of the green beans that is requires for this season. The options are agree a price at the beginning of the year, buy at the going rate later in the year, or buy half at a predetermined rate and half later in the year. Prices later in the year will depend upon the season as shown in the table below. If the table below also shows the probabilities associated with the different types of season and the

cost of beans per kilograms associated with the different strategies, which is the company's optimum strategy under the expected value criterion? Would the application of the minimax criterion lead to a different decision?

Season	Prob of Season	Strategy		
		Buy Now	*Buy Later*	*Buy Half Now*
Good	0.3	20	12	16
Fair	0.4	20	22	21
Poor	0.3	20	28	24

Probability

1. Thirty chief executive officers in a certain industry are classified by age and by their previous functional position as shown in the table below:

Previous Position	Age		
	Under 55	*55 and Older*	*Total*
Finance	4	14	18
Marketing	1	5	6
Other	4	2	6
Total	9	21	30

Suppose an executive is selected at random from this group.

a. What is the probability that the executive chosen is under 55? What type of probability is this?

b. What is the probability that an executive chosen at random is 55 or older and with Marketing as previous functional position? What type of probability is this?

c. Suppose an executive is selected, and you are told that the previous position was in Finance. What is the probability that the executive is under 55? What kind of probability is this?

d. Are age and previous position independent factors for this group of executives?

2. Records of service requests at a garage and their probabilities are as follows:

Daily demand	Probability
5	.3
6	.7

Daily demand is independent. What is the probability that over a two day period the number of requests will be:

a. 10 requests
b. 11 requests
c. 12 requests.

3. Which of the following probability distributions would be objective and which subjective?

a. number of sixes in 5000 tosses of a fair die

b. number of prosperous years in the next 10 years

c. the probability that IBM will return a profit in each of the next five years

d. the probability of drawing the name of a male doctor randomly from tic list of members of the British Medical Association.

Expected Values

1. The following probabilities are assigned to the possible values of the fraction defective in a manufacturing process. Compute the expected value of the random variable fraction defective.

Event (% defective)	Probability of Event
.01	.10
.02	.15
.03	.20
.04	.30
.05	.20
.10	.03
.15	.02

2. A gardening contractor can not work in heavy rain, and only works at 50% efficiency in light rain. A job is taken on that will take 65 hours to complete if the weather remains fair. Given that the probability of heavy rain is 0.2 and the probability of light rain is 0.3, how long is it likely to take the contractor to finish the job?

3. A sales manager lists the following probabilities for various demand levels for a new product.

Probability	Demand(units)
.1	50
.3	100
.3	150
.15	200
.10	250
.05	300

Suppose that the cost of introducing the product is £5,000 which needs to be set against the profit and profit per unit is £50. What is the total expected profit from the new product?

8

Decision Trees

Objectives

When you have read this chapter you should:

- be familiar with the basic structure of a decision tree;
- be capable of applying simple methods for developing decision trees;
- appreciate why financial concepts such as Net Present Value may need to be used in decision trees;
- understand the significance of probabilities in decision trees;
- appreciate that different decision criteria can be applied to analyse decision trees.

What is a Decision Tree?

In most organisations managers do not deal with decisions in isolation. They think ahead to the next decision, and probably consider several rounds of subsequent decisions and the potential outcomes. Decision trees are a techniques that may assist in representing such a series of decisions and thereby help the decision maker to analyse situations more clearly.

A decision tree is a graphical tool for describing:

- the strategies available to a decision maker;
- the events that can occur, and;
- the relationships between the strategies and events.

A decision tree may contain similar data to that summarised in a pay-off table, but offers a different way of working through the options, and is particularly appropriate when the decision maker needs to make a series of decisions, one of which may lead to another, possibly over an extended period of time. The objective of a decision tree is to structure the decision problem and to help the manager to find a solution.

The Structure of a Decision Tree

The basic structure of a decision tree is always the same. Below a simple model is shown. This incorporates

- Strategies,
- Events, and
- Conditional Profit.

The first two of these, strategies and events, may appear more than once. For example, the tree may be structured: Strategies, Events, Strategies, Events, Conditional Profit. Figure 8.1 shows the basic structure of a decision tree.

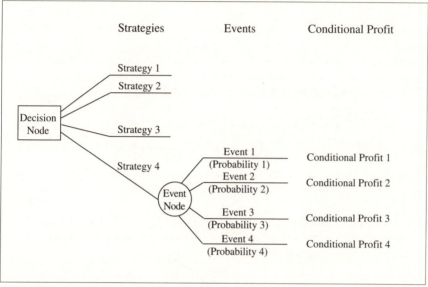

Figure 8.1: Basic Structure of a Decision Tree

Considering Figure 8.1, we can see that the basic structure of a decision tree reflects a series of decisions and events. Starting at the left hand side, there is a decision node. Emanating from this decision node are possible strategies that may be adopted as a result of that decision. Decisions associated with a decision node are under the control of the decision maker. If a specified strategy is chosen, then one of a number of events may occur. These potential events are shown emanating form the event node. Events are beyond the control of the decision maker. In this figure the only event node displayed is that associated with Strategy 4, in the interests of simplicity. Clearly there would also be event nodes associated with each strategy. In general, then, if a strategy is chosen, and an event occurs, a conditional profit can be associated with each combination of strategy and event. This is shown in the final column of Figure 8.1.

With only one decision node and only one event node, the decision tree shows no more than might be summarised in a pay-off table. You may like to try displaying the data in Example 7.2 as a simple decision tree.

Decision trees are particularly valuable when a manager wishes to view a series of decision nodes and event nodes, so that the tree has, for example, a general structure:

Strategies - Events - Strategies - Events - Conditional Profit

The strategies and events elements may be repeated as many times as there are decision nodes. Typically, then, decision trees can be used to represent a series of decisions, one of which follows from another. They reflect the approach:

'If we do this, that might happen, then we would have to decide between these options, but then these other events might happen. What will be the best initial decision given the range of possible outcomes?'

It is important to note, before we move on to consider in more detail the mechanics of the development of decision trees, that they are only a technique for evaluating a series of strategies. In order to construct a real decision tree we need to have considerable information concerning the decision environments and consequences. For examples, it is necessary to know:

1. What are the appropriate available strategies?
2. What other events should be seriously considered?
3. What are the subjective probabilities of each of these events happening?
4. What is the conditional profit associated with each of the outcomes?

Decision trees, like all models are simplifications and abstractions of the real problem. Judgement must be applied in order to assess what to include and in order to estimate the probabilities of the various events.

Building a Decision Tree

The construction of a decision tree involves two phases: the forward pass and the backward pass.

The forward pass builds the structure of the decision tree considering the decisions to be made, the events that might occur, and their sequence. Although it is normal to complete the process by then applying the backward pass, even this initial analysis can often be useful on its own. The forward pass can be viewed as a useful means of clarifying the issues, identifying possible strategies, considering possible events, and indicating the information that is required in order to evaluate all of the strategies. The backward pass examines the expected monetary values associated with each set of event branches, and by so doing enables the decision maker to identify the optimum strategy.

Forward Pass (Moving Forward)

The forward pass involves the decision maker in identifying the decisions to be made, the events that might occur and the sequence of decisions and events. The forward pass reveals the structure of the problem. During the forward pass conditional profits must be calculated (i.e. the profits that will be achieved if certain strategies are adopted and certain events occur) and the probability of events must be assessed.

Backward Pass

The backward pass is concerned with analysing the decision problem. Expected values are estimated by working backwards through the tree.

- For each set of event branches the expected value is calculated.
- For each set of decision branches the one with the highest expected value is selected.
- The strategy with the highest expected value is selected and a \\ is drawn through lines representing the other options

The final analysis should lead to a decision. Once this decision has been identified, a preferred strategy will emerge. In addition to the identification of the preferred strategy, tracing through the tree will yield a more complete picture. For example, a decision tree may show that a product should be marketed, and also that it may be appropriate to charge a high price if there is no competitive entry, but a medium price if there is competition.

Example 8.1 : A Simple Example of a Decision Tree

Figure 8.2 shows the development of a decision tree for a specific example where a company must decide whether or not to introduce a new product into the market place, and if they do introduce the product the price level of the product. Clearly events that may befall the company are that a competitor may enter the marketplace, and that the competitor, also, has a choice concerning the price level of his product. Whether or not a competitor enters the market may influence the optimum strategy for the company.

Figure 8.2(a) shows the forward pass through the decision tree during which the strategies and events are enumerated, with probabilities attached to the events. Clearly, in practice the identification of the options, possible events and probabilities involves a great deal of judgement and collation of the correct information.

Figure 8.2(b) shows the backward pass through the decision tree during which the expected values of each strategy are evaluated, and the optimum strategy identified.

We examine the forward pass and the backward pass in more detail.

Forward Pass

The forward pass starts by identifying the strategies available to the decision maker and the events that might occur. The two decisions are:

1. Whether to market the product or not;
2. The level at which to set the price.

The events are:

1. A competitor may or may not introduce a competitive product
2. A competitor may price the product at a low, medium or high price.

The decision tree must reflect the order in which decisions must be made. For example, the manager may be able to decide to market the product, but leave the setting of the price until the competitor's reaction is evident, or, alternatively, may need to set the price at the same time as deciding to market. Here we assume that the company can decide to introduce the product and announce it, wait a short while to discover whether a competitor will enter the market place, then set the price level. After this,the competitor will announce their price. This sequence of decisions and events is shown in Figure 8.2. The decision tree must reflect the sequence of decisions and events in the decision making process.

To complete the forward pass through the tree, it is necessary to estimate the conditional profit for every combination of actions and events. Also the probabilities for each event must be assessed by the decision maker. These probabilities may depend on prior actions or events. In this example, we assume that the decision maker has estimated both the conditional profits and the probabilities of events, but we will return to how these might be estimated in Example 8.2.

Backward Pass

To analyse the decision problem and to identify the optimum strategy we work backwards through the decision tree.

For each set of event branches an expected value (EV) is calculated, and for each set of decision branches the one with he highest EV is selected. This is shown in Figure 8.3, for our example. First the EV are calculated for the event nodes associated with the competitors price. For example, the EV of 5 in the top right circle in Figure 8.3 represents the sum of the product of the probabilities for high, medium and low prices times the respective conditional profits:

$$EV = (0.3)(150) + (0.5)(0) + (0.2)(-200) = 5$$

The values shown in the other event nodes are calculated similarly.

Now we move back to the decision node and select, from the event nodes, the strategy which appears to be the most attractive on the basis of a comparison of the event nodes. If we choose the strategy with the highest expected profit, then we select the strategy Set Medium Price. We draw a // through the non-preferred strategies and record the value 110 in the decision node box.

When no competitors product is introduced, the best choice is a high price with a profit of £400,000.

We then calculate the EV of the next event node in a similar manner to earlier calculations for event nodes, i.e.

$$EV = (0.7)(110) + (0.3)(400) = 197$$

We then examine the values of the two event nodes associated with the first decision node. The expected profit if the product is introduced is £197,000, whereas if it is not it is 0.

The decision tree not only suggests the first decision which is to introduce the product, but also suggests the following strategies:

- Introduce the product and charge a high price if there is no competitive product
- Introduce the product and charge a medium price if there is a competitive product.

Some Points To Remember About Decision Trees

1. The decision tree should be structured in such a way that the events from an event node must be mutually exclusive so that only one of them can happen at any one time. If events are mutually exclusive, the sum of their probabilities will equal 1.

2. All branches emanating from any node must be the same logical type. The decision maker needs to distinguish between those decisions that are under his control and those that are not.

3. The strategies associated with a decision tree must include all of the acceptable alternatives under consideration. If alternatives are overlooked important options may not be considered. There may , on the other hand, be alternative strategies that have been ruled out on environmental, political, legal, or other grounds and these will not be shown.

4. All events that are considered likely must be reflected. Again, the decision maker must exercise judgement in determining what are likely events, and there may be events whose probability is too low to consider seriously, and these will be omitted.

5. Probabilities may be conditional and their calculation may be more complex than in our early simple examples. We consider this in more detail in Example 8.2.

6. The conditional outcomes may require considerable data collection and analysis before the forward pass can be completed. Since decisions may be spread over time, techniques such as net present value may be used to assist in the calculation of outcomes. This is also considered further in Example 8.2

7. Expected value is an easy criterion to apply when first considering decision trees, but it is not appropriate in all circumstances. First, we have tended to use expected monetary value, and to express outcomes in monetary terms. There are many circumstances where outcomes need to be expressed in non-financial terms. For instance, an advertising campaign manager may be concerned to select a strategy that will yield maximum exposure of product or service. A hospital manager may be concerned to minimise the time that patients have to wait for operations after diagnosis. In such instances we can construct a decision tree that uses the expected value of an appropriate variable. In Chapter 7, however, we saw that outcomes may be evaluated on the basis of a range of different decision criteria. Again, in a decision tree, we may choose one of these alternative criteria. In Chapter 9 we consider the concept of utility which may be appropriate as a decision criterion where the risks are large, and again, may also be used in decision trees.

Example 8.2

This example allows us to explore some of the complexities associated with decision trees. In Example 8.1, we assumed that the manager had calculated conditional profits and the probabilities of events. Here we investigate how these might be derived, and demonstrate that there are a number of important issues to be considered in this process.

A pharmaceutical company has produced and conducted preliminary laboratory trials on a new vitamin tablet called Everwell. Before Everwell can be marketed it must undergo:

- further laboratory trials;
- clinical trials, and;
- a launch.

The company has to make three decisions in the order given below:

- Whether to conduct laboratory trials or abandon the product;
- Whether to conduct clinical trials or abandon the product;
- Whether to launch the product onto the marker or abandon it.

Figure 8.3 indicates the basic structure of the decision tree that will model this decision process. Laboratory trials can show the product to be good, moderate or bad,. Clinical trials can be Positive or Neutral, and the Launch can be a success or a failure. Notice that even this relatively simple problem starts to generate a relatively complex tree. This demonstrates the limitations of decision trees as drawn on a sheet of paper in this form, although they can be subdivided into sub trees. It also demonstrates the number of combinations of strategies and events that a decision maker should be considering and the difficulty that they are likely to encounter in thoroughly considering all options without some structured approach such as a decision tree to help to analyse the problem. Admittedly, some of the options shown on this tree may be rejected, but we retain them all here for completeness. For example, if the laboratory trials outcome was Bad, we might not proceed to a clinical trial.

Calculating Conditional Profits

Each branch has an associated return. Since the objective is to discover he best strategy, we only need to consider marginal costs. Costs, such as overheads which are incurred regardless of the decision that is made are applicable to all strategies and whilst they may be important to the financial health of the organisation, they can be ignored in the decision tree. Often a fairly rough estimate of cost is the best that can be offered, and may anyway be sufficient to differentiate between the strategies.

Typically, in a decision tree, events may take time. Here, for example, laboratory trials will take a year. Over one year it may not be essential to take into account the 'time effect of money, but certainly for longer periods this must be a consideration when calculating outcomes. A sum spent at the end of the year actually costs less than the same sum spent at the beginning of the year, if only because it could have been invested in the meantime and earned some interest. Formally it is possible to discount all costs and values to the present, so that fair comparisons can be made. The procedure is known as net present value (NPV). We introduce a simple approach to NPV here. In NPV, cash flows are assumed to occur at a particular point in time, usually at the end of the year, and are discounted to the present by what is termed 'an agreed minimum earnings rate'. This is the rate of return that a company would expect to have on capital investment projects.

Suppose, then, that the company here decides on a discount rate of 10 per cent, and makes the assumption that half of the costs of the further laboratory trials will be incurred at the beginning of the year, and the remainder at the end. If the laboratory trials cost £50,000, then:

$$\text{NPV for laboratory trials} = 25,000 + 25,000/1.1$$
$$= £47,727$$

Clinical trials will take three years, and these take place after laboratory trials have ended, that is in Years 2,3, and 4. Estimated costs are £150,000, £175,000 and £200,000, respectively. If these costs are incurred at the beginning of the corresponding years, then:

$$\text{NPV for clinical trials} = £150,000/(1.1) + £175,000/(1.1)^2 + £200,000(1.1)^3$$
$$= £431,255$$

Another cost involved in the project is the cost of the launch. The estimated cost of the launch is £500,000. This will be incurred in four year's time. Discounted at the same rate this amounts to:

$$\text{NPV for launch} = 500{,}000/(1.1)^4 = £341507.$$

The final figure is the value of the return when the product's success or lack of it becomes evident. Given that we are looking at a return that might take place over several years and will not commence until four or more years from the present, there is inevitably some subjectivity associated with the calculation of these outcomes. Assume that we place a figure on this of £5,000,000 if the product is successful and £2,000,000 if the product is a failure. Discounting these to the present time, the figures are £3,415,067 and £1,366,027, respectively.

We can now place costs on all appropriate branches of the tree and, thereby, estimate the conditional pay-offs associated with each branch, by taking the costs into account.

The main reason for working through each of these options is to demonstrates that much data must be collected concerning the costs of various decisions, and various financial assumptions must be made before conditional profits can be calculated.

Probabilities

Clearly most of the probabilities used in a decision tree are subjective. In this example, we review probabilities for each of the sets of events associated with the outcomes of the laboratory trials, clinical trials and market success.

The issues are complicated by the fact that the probabilities are unlikely to be independent. Indeed they are likely to be conditional. For example, if further laboratory trials produces a good result, the probability of a positive result from clinical trials is better than when the laboratory trial result is moderate or bad.

Whilst it may be relatively easy to offer an estimate of the probability that Everwell will be commercially viable, or the probability for the various combined outcomes for the laboratory trials and for the clinical trials given that the economic viability is assured, the answers to these questions generate conditional probabilities (given success, what is the probability of a successful clinical trial?) In the decision tree we require marginal probabilities. In order to generate such probabilities it would be necessary to be able to answer questions such as:

- What is the probability that Everwell is successful, given that the clinical trails were positive, and that the laboratory trials gave a Moderate result?

Such probabilities are difficult to estimate, and we are often required to calculate them from the conditional probabilities that the decision maker may be more able to supply.

Suppose that in our example we assign the following letters to the events or outcomes, so that we can represent the probabilities clearly:

G effectiveness good
M effectiveness moderate
B effectiveness bad
P clinical trial positive
N clinical trail neutral
S market success
F market failure.

Looking at the tree in Figure 8.3 we can see that we require the probabilities: $P(G)$, $P(M)$, $P(B)$, and then for the next set of branches, $P(P/G)$, $P(N/G)$, $P(P/M)$, $P(N/M)$, $P(P/B)$ and $P(P/B)$. For the final stage we require: $P(S/PG)$ $P(F/PG)$, $P(S/NG)$, $P(F/NG)$, $P(S/PM)$, $P(F/PM)$, $P(S/NM)$, $P(F/NM)$. $P(S/PB)$, $P(F/PB)$, $P(S/NB)$ and $P(F/NB)$).

We have already observed that collecting such conditional probabilities may present problems. For example the decision maker may seek to estimate first of all the probability of market success or failure; these are assigned values of $P(S) = 0.7$ and $P(F) = 0.3$. Then the decision maker estimates the probabilities of, for example, the various combined outcomes for the laboratory trials and the clinical trial, given that the substance will be a market success. The same questions are then asked for some similar substance which is known to be a failure.

The results of the questions are tabulated below:

Given Market Outcome	*Outcomes of Trials*					
	PG	NG	PM	NM	PB	NB
Success(S)	0.40	0.15	0.20	0.10	0.10	0.05
Failure(F)	0.05	0.10	0.10	0.20	0.20	0.35

This table shows conditional probabilities of the form $P(PG/S)$, but we required conditional probabilities in the opposite direction. These can be derived using the laws of probability (see the end of Chapter 7).

The initial probabilities such as $P(G)$ can be derived if we note that P and N are mutually exclusive events, and that G occurs only if either G and P occurs or if G and N occurs. Thus by the addition law:

$$P(G) = P(PG) + P(NG)$$

using the law of total probabilities

$$P(G) = P(PG/S)\ P(S) + P(PG/F)P(F) + P(NG/S)P(S) + P(NG/F)P(F).$$

Thus we can calculate $P(G)$ from the probabilities offered by the decision maker.

Finally in the intermediate stage, by the multiplication law:

$$P(P/G) = P(PG) / P(G)$$
$$= \frac{P(PG/S)P(S) + P(PG/F)P(F)}{P(G)}$$

Here again the expression is in terms that were given initially. Using these formulae it is possible to calculate the probabilities in the table below:

G	M	B	P/G	N/G	P/M	N/M	P/B	N/B
0.430	0.300	0.270	0.686	0.314	0.567	0.433	0.481	0.519

S/PG	F/PG	S/NG	F/NG	S/PM	F/PM	S/NM	F/NM	S/PB
0.949	0.051	0.778	0.222	0.824	0.176	0.538	0.462	0.538

F/PB	S/NB	F/NB
0.462	0.250	0.750

The identification of these probabilities can present problems. It can be difficult to estimate the likely success of a product. Decision trees must therefore be constructed on the basis of best guess. In the absence of a decision tree, the decision maker would make decisions intuitively. Although decision trees must inevitably incorporate may estimates, they, at least impose the discipline of asking the decision maker to think quantitatively.

Decision Criteria in the Backward Pass

In our previous discussion we have used the expected value criterion as a means of evaluating the options in the backward pass. We will first demonstrate how this might be used in evaluating this decision tree and then consider other decision criteria that might also be appropriate.

To apply the expected value criterion, we start at the event node in the top right hand corner. The expected value at this node is:

$$(0.949)(2594578) + (0.051)(2186516) = 2350,742$$

The value of the abandon action is negative, and therefore, at the decision node the strategy would be to launch, and the value at the decision node would be 2,350,742. Other nodes can be calculated similarly and are shown in Figure 8.4.

Other decision criteria could also be applied. For example, if we consider the Minimax Criterion, this asks us to look for the strategy with the smallest possible loss, or the largest minimum profit. Here, any abandonment of the project other than at the beginning, will be more costly than initial abandonment. The only relevant factor then is whether the project is successful. If it is then, with hindsight, the best strategy is to launch, and if it is not successful, the best strategy is to abandon before any trials. In summary, the criterion says that since the company stands to gain more by a successful project than it would lose by failure, the product should always be launched. Clearly, this criterion is not sufficiently discriminating to be taken seriously.

Another criterion that we might use is the equally likely criterion, where we assume that all events are equally likely. This requires us to be discriminating as to which strategies are plausible and which are not. Since the probabilities of all of the events are equal, the probability of any given event is determined by the number of plausible events. In order to apply this criteria we need to decide how many strategies are plausible, and this may resent some problems.

Sensitivity Analysis

Throughout the construction of the decision tree model we have used estimates: estimates for the probabilities of events and estimates for the conditional profits and other costs. It is therefore reasonable to investigate the extent to which the recommendations for a preferred strategy would change if different estimates were used. This can be achieved by investigating the range of values of a probability, or of a cost over which a certain strategy would remain optimal. Simple models look at the sensitivity of the solution to changes in just one variable. More complex, computer-based models may allow an investigation of the effect of simultaneous changes in two or more variables.

Conclusion

Decision trees are useful graphical tools which can be used to represent a series of decisions and to help the decision maker to analyse situations where they are faced with sequential decisions. The basic structure of a decision tree includes strategies, events, and conditional profits. The construction of a decision tree involves two phases: the forward pass and the backward pass. The forward pass helps to identify the structure of the decision making situation. The backward pass applies a decision criterion in order to attempt to evaluate the best strategy. A decision tree, in common with any other model is an abstraction and simplification of the real world and the decision maker must carefully identify key decisions and key events for inclusion in the tree.

The calculation of the conditional profits may require considerable data collection and analysis and may need to take into account the effect of time, by using techniques such as Net Present Value. The probabilities of the events in a decision tree are often conditional, and may need to be calculated from other simple probabilities. Although expected value is widely used as a decision criterion in decision trees, it may not always be the most appropriate decision rule, and other options can also be considered.

Review Questions

1. In what way does the basic structure of a decision tree reflect the design making process in many businesses?
2. What does a forward pass in a decision tree achieve?
3. What does a backward pass in a decision tree achieve?
4. What are the limitations of expected value as a decision criterion in a decision tree?
5. Why are concepts such as conditional and marginal probability relevant in the construction of decision trees?
6. Why might sensitivity analysis be used in decision trees?
7. What is the difference between an event node and a decision node?
8. Why is it necessary to introduce the concept of Net Present Value in decision trees?

Case Study Questions

Note: These Questions do not require you to use concepts such as Net Present Value, and Conditional Probabilities

1. A company has the opportunity to market a new service. Initially, it has two possible courses of action: to test market on a limited scale or to give up the project completely. A test market would cost £160,000 and current evidence suggests that customer reaction is equally likely to be positive or negative. If the reaction to the test marketing were to be positive, the company could either market the service nationally, or still give up the project completely. Research suggests that a national launch might result in the following sales

Sales	Contribution(£m)	Probability
High	1.2	0.25
Average	0.3	0.5
Low	-0.24	0.25

If the test marketing were to yield negative results the company would give up the project. It is anticipated that giving up the project would result in a contribution of £60,000 from the sale of the right to offer the service to a second party. All contributions have been discounted to present values.

(a) Draw a decision tree to represent the situation, including all relevant probabilities and financial values.

(b) Recommend a course of action for the company, on the basis of the expected value decision criterion.
(c) Explain any limitations inherent in this method of analysis.

2. A company is trying to decide about the size of a new plant. At present the company has only a minimal sales effort, but when the new plant is completed a major promotion effort will be undertaken. Management is somewhat uncertain about the likely success of this effort. It is estimated that there is a 0.3 chance that the company will capture a significant market share, and a 0.7 chance that it will capture a moderate market share. A larger plant will be necessary if a significant market share is captured. A small plant would suffice if the market share were only moderate. The large plant costs £8m, the small plant costs £5m.

If a significant market share emerges, the estimated value of resulting profits (excluding the cost of the plant) is £14m; if a moderate share is achieved, the present value of the resulting profits is £9m.

Management has one other alternative. They could build a small plant, wait to see the level of sales, and then expand the plant if the situation warrants. It would cost an additional £4.5m to expand the small plant.

(a) Draw a decision tree for this problem.
(b) What decision should the company make?, What is its expected value?

3. A firm has developed a new product. They can either subject the product to a market test or abandon it at this stage. Market tests cost £50,000. It is estimated that there is a 0.7 chance of success and a 0.3 chance of failure as a result of the market test. If the market test is favourable they could either continue, and launch the product or abandon the project. If the product is marketed possible levels of demand are likely to realise:

Demand	Probability	Amount
Low	0.3	-£50,000
Medium	0.6	£250,000
High	0.1	£550,000

Against these profits must be set the cost of the market test.

If the test market indicates failure the project would be abandoned. Abandonment at any stage realises £30,000 from sale of machinery.

(a) Draw the decision tree to model the strategies open to the company.
(b) Use the decision tree to help you to recommend a course of action. Which decision criterion do you feel might be appropriate in these circumstances?
(c) Are there any assumptions embedded in this decision tree that might limit the applicability of this analysis?

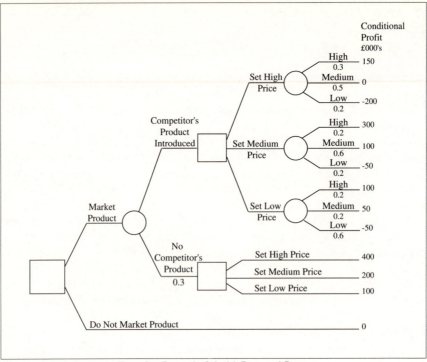

Figure 8.2: A Decision Tree for Example 8.1 (a) Forward Pass

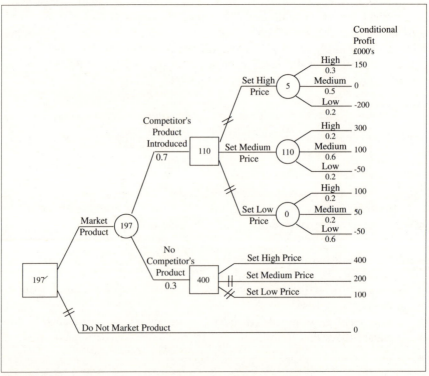

Figure 8.2: A Decision Tree for Example 8.1 (b) Backward Pass

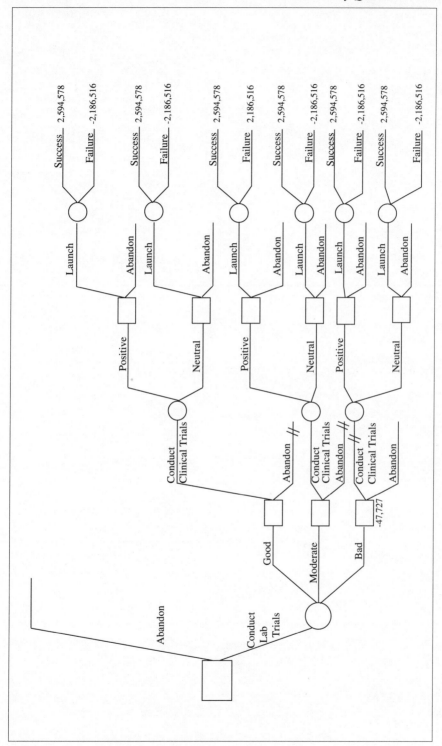

Figure 8.3: A Decision Tree for Example 8.2

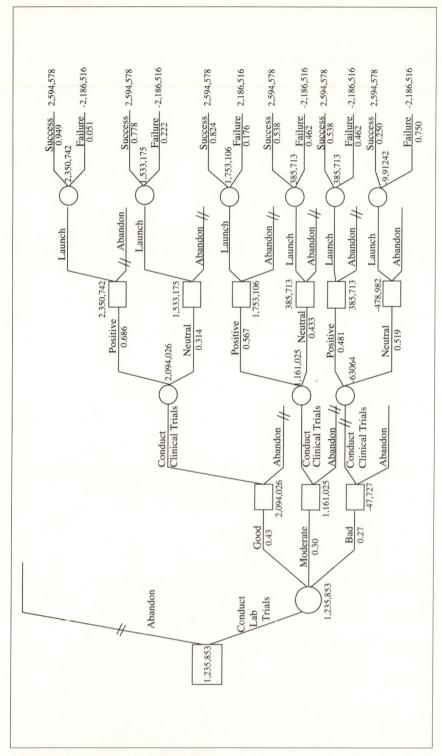

Figure 8.4: A Decision Tree for Example 8.2

9

Risk Taking and Utility

Objectives

The concepts in this Chapter are concerned with the decision makers attitude to risk, and approaches that allow this to be taken into account in the decision making process. When you have read this chapter you will:

- appreciate the value of utility in reflecting the decision makers' attitude to risk;
- understand the concepts of utility and utility functions;
- be able to construct your own utility function in order to be able to assess your attitude to risk in specific situations;
- have an awareness of the concepts of certainty equivalents and risk premiums.

Introduction

In the last two chapters we have used expected value as a decision criterion in order to select between two or more strategies. Yet in some circumstances, expected value is not an appropriate decision criterion. It does not suggest the strategy that a wise manager might adopt. This is particularly likely to be the case for decisions that are one off and involve large amounts of money. Some decision makers would prefer to be more cautious than might be suggested by the expected value criterion, and others might be prepared to take a larger risk in the hope of large gains. Utility is an alternative concept to expected value, which was proposed as a means of catering for the fact that maximising expected monetary value does not always lead to a course of action that the experienced decision maker would select. When the decision maker rejects the expected value criterion it is asserted that individuals make decisions to maximize expected utility. The concept of utility takes into account the decision makers attitude to risk. In order to demonstrate that the decision makers' attitude to risk is important consider the following simple example:

Example 9.1

You have a choice between A1 or A2 and B1 or B2. Which of A1 or A2 or B1 or B2 would you choose?:

A1: Certainty of £100,000

A2: On the flip of a fair coin, Heads you get £0, tails you get £250,000

B1: No gain or loss

B2: One chance out of one hundred of incurring a £9000 debt, and a 99 out of a 100 chance of winning £100

Most people choose A1 and B1, in preference, respectively to A2 and B2, but the highest expected value is associated with A2 and B2, since :

- the expected value of A1 is £100,000 and
- the expected value of A2 is $0.5 \times 0 + 0.5 \times £250,000 = £125,000$, and
- the expected value of B1 is £0,
- and the expected value of B2 is $0.01 \times £9000 + 0.99 \times £100 = £9$

We might say then that A1 and B1 have a higher utility for the decision maker than A2 and B2. In circumstances such as these where the risks are high, expected value is not a good decision criterion. It does not lead to decisions that would be chosen by the wise decision maker, nor does it accommodate the differing attitudes to risk that different individuals may have.

Measuring Utility

Expected value is easy to calculate and is unambiguous and independent of individual decision makers and therefore has significant attractions. Expected utility (EU) is not so easy to measure. It is different for different decision makers, depending on the decision makers' attitude to risk in the circumstances that surround a specific decision. Also it may not be possible always to assign a numerical value to utility, but only to evaluate one decision as having greater or less utility than another decision. Utility is often represented by a utility function for a given decision maker. This utility function reflects the choices that a decision maker would make over a range of different monetary values. It is possible to assess a person's utility function by observing a series of real or hypothetical decisions that are made by that decision maker.

In starting to measure anything we need to consider the possible different scales that might be used to measure them, especially since it may not always be possible to allocate a numerical value to utility.

Scales

We have already indicated that utility may be an elusive concept to measure. We may not always be able to assign numerical values to the utility of a given decision, and so it is necessary to consider the three possible types of scales that may be used to measure utility. These scales are:

Nominal or classification scale

A nominal or classification scale assigns a description to a set of elements. This description can be a number or an adjective. Using this kind of scale strategies could be classified as having negative utility or positive utility, but a nominal scale offers no ordering or ranking.

Ordinal Measure

An ordinal measure adds relative ordering or ranking to different values of utility. Objects can be seen as being more or less than other objects. Ordinal measures of utility are used in analysing situations with riskless choices.

An indifference curve that displays decisions between which the decision maker is indifferent can be built in order to collect alternatives with equal utility, and then we can compare these alternatives with equal utility with the choices on another indifference curve that is higher (or more desirable) or lower (and less desirable).

Cardinal measure

Using a cardinal measure a number is assigned that is an interval measure of a characteristic e.g. distance in feet. The von Neumann-Morgenstern measure of utility is a special type of cardinal measure which measures utility in situations involving risk to the decision maker. Any utility function sums up a person's attitude towards risk.

Psychological Assumptions

There are some psychological assumptions underlying a person's attitude to risk that must be made for successful and accurate application of the concept of utility and utility functions. It will become apparent why these assumptions are necessary as we start to use the concept in subsequent sections. These assumptions are:

1. With any two alternatives, we can decide whether we are indifferent between them, or which one we prefer.
2. Alternatives are transitive. In other words if:

A is preferred to B, and B is preferred to C, then A is preferred to C.

Note that although this is usually the case, the choices may be intransitive if the degree of preference between choices is slight.

So, for example, if you were offered a choice between three different holiday destinations: Paris, California or Sydney, you may prefer Sydney to California and California to Paris. Transitivity assumes that you would then prefer Sydney to Paris. However, if the degree of preference between choices were slight, transitivity might not hold, and you may, in fact prefer Paris to Sydney.

3. If a person is indifferent between two strategies or lotteries, i.e. each would be equally acceptable — then one lottery can be substituted for the first if this makes the analysis easier.

4. If two lotteries have the same two possible outcomes, but the outcomes have different probabilities, then the lottery with the more favourable outcome having the higher probability is the preferred lottery.

Example 9.2

To illustrate the above point, suppose that you have to choose between the lotteries A and B in the table below. The possible outcomes are the same in both lotteries, but the probabilities associated with those outcomes vary between A and B

	Prob of Outcomes	
Possible Outcomes	A	B
£1000	0.8	0.5
£0	0.2	0.5

Under this assumption, here A is preferred to B because the probability of achieving the higher return is higher. Note that another way of viewing this situation is in terms of probabilistic dominance and we might, for instance, say that A dominates B by probabilistic dominance.

5. If A is preferred to B, and B preferred to C, then there is some lottery involving A and C that is indifferent to B for certain.

B is called the certainty equivalent of the lottery. We return to the concept of certainty equivalents later.

6. If A is preferred to B and there is some third alternative C, then any lottery involving A and C is preferred to a corresponding lottery of B and C, provided that the probability of assignments are the same in both lotteries. It is required that the probability attached to C be less than one.

Example 9.3

To illustrate this point, take a lottery involving A and C, where
- A: offers a 0.6 probability of £1000
- B: offers a 0.4 probability of £400
- C: offers a 0.4 probability of £0

Now clearly A has a higher expected value than B, and therefore may be preferred to B depending on how good an indication of the decision makers' attitude expected value is.

This assumption says that since A is preferred to B any lottery involving A and C is preferred to a corresponding lottery involving B and C.

7. The utility of a lottery is defined to be equal to the expectation of the utilities of its components. Thus if, for example, a lottery can be viewed as comprising component lotteries, then we can calculate the utility of the main lottery.

This assumption is useful if we wish to engage in any mathematical manipulation.

The utility of a lottery L_1 can be expressed in terms of its outcomes thus:

$$U(L_1) = p_1 U(A_1) + p_2 U(A_2) ... + p_n U(A_n).$$

where $U(L_1)$ is the utility of lottery L_1,
and p_1 are the probabilities of the possible outcomes
and $U(A_i)$ are the utilities of the various outcomes.

Where there are only two component lotteries L_1 and L_2 of the lottery L and the lotteries L_1 and L_2 themselves have a probability of occurrence r and $(1-r)$ respectively, then;

$$U(L) = r \, U(L_1) + (1-r)U(L_2)$$

Example 9.4

The table below summarises the outcomes from two component lotteries of the lottery L, L_1 and L_2. We would like to use assumption 7 to calculate the utility of lottery L, given that we know the utilities of the component lotteries. This can be achieved thus:

Lottery	Outcomes	Utility of Outcomes	Prob
L_1	$\{$ 1000	50	0.6
	0	0	0.4
L_2	400	40	1.0

From this table

$$U(L_1) = 0.6 \times 50 + 0.4 \times 0 = 30$$

$$U(L_2) = 1.0 \times 40 = 40$$

If probability of $L_1 = 0.8$ and probability of $L_2 = 0.2$,
then the expected utility of the lottery L is:

$$U(L) = 0.8 \times 30 + 0.2 \times 40 = 32.$$

Utility Functions

Utility functions represent the subjective attitude of a decision maker to risk. They summarise the decision makers' attitude to risk over a range of values, which are often expressed in monetary terms. Such a function can be used to evaluate decision alternatives involving uncertain outcomes. Often we assess a person's utility function in monetary terms but we could look as other value systems. Here we use money as a basis for our measures.

The General Shape of Utility Functions

Some generalisations concerning the general shape of utility functions are possible. People usually regard money as a desirable commodity, and the utility of a large sum is usually greater than the utility of a smaller sum. Generally a utility function has a positive slope over an appropriate range of money values, and the slope probably does not vary in response to small changes in the stock of money. For small changes in the amount of money going to an individual the slope is constant and the utility function is linear. If the utility function is linear, the decision maker maximises expected utility by maximising expected monetary value. However, for large variations in the amount of money this is unlikely to be the case. For large losses and large gains the utility function often approaches upper and lower limits. The slope of the curve will usually increase sharply as the amount of loss increases, because the disutility of a large loss is proportionately more than the disutility of a small loss, but the curve will flatten as the loss becomes very large. Similarly for large stocks of money, the slope of the utility function grows smaller with further additions of that stock. This is consistent with a decision maker who is risk adverse. The risk adverse decision maker has a utility function of the general shape shown in Figure 9.1. For a risk adverse decision maker, the expected utility of a lottery is less than the utility of the expected monetary value.

It is also possible for the decision maker to be risk preferring, at least over some range of the utility function. In this case the expected utility of a lottery is more than the utility of the expected monetary value. Figure 9.1 shows a risk preferring function.

On this graph, a person maximises utility by maximising EMV. Therefore EMV may be a useful decision criterion in the range in which the utility function is linear.

But, when there are large variations in the amount of money, i.e. large losses or gains at issue, the utility function ceases to be linear, and starts to look like one of the functions below.

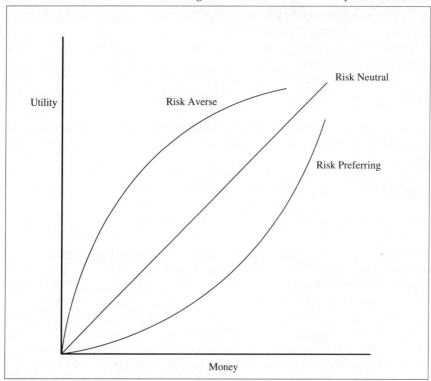

Figure 9.1: Utility Functions

Assessing a Decision Maker's Utility Function

You can assess your own or someone else's utility function, by assessing your attitude to a series of different lotteries. This would be necessary if you wished to reflect your attitude towards risk in a decision situation where large losses or profits were at stake. The points below demonstrate how you might start to go through this process.

1. Start by identifying two values as reference points, and then build up other points in between by considering alternatives to which you are indifferent.

Choose say U(-£10,000) = 0 and U (£100,000) = 1.0 as reference points.

2. Formulate lottery A_1 that offers 0.5 probability of -£10,000 and 0.5 probability of £100,000.

i.e. $U(A_1) = 0.5U(-£10,000) + 0.5U(£100,000)$
 $= 0.5 \times 0 + 0.5 \times 1.0$
 $= 0.5$

3. Now formulate some alternative to the lottery A_1, A_2 that yields some money with certainty, say £25,000.

4. Now choose between A_1 and A_2.

If you choose A then:

$$U(A_2) > U(A_1) = 0.5$$

5. Continue thus with different A_2's until you find an alternative that is as attractive to you as A_1.

Then

$$U(A_2) = U(A_1) = 0.5$$

Suppose that this is the alternative that offers £15,000 for certain, then:

$$U(£15,000) = 0.5.$$

This can then be plotted as an additional point on your utility function.

6. Now add another point to the utility function by posing another set of alternatives, but again based on the points whose utility is known:

A_3 : offers a 0.5 probability of £15,000 and a 0.5 probability of £100,000.

Try to identify the certain sum equivalent as previously — say this is £47,000 for a given decision maker for this lottery A_3.

$$\text{So } U(47,000) = 0.5U(15,000) + 0.5U(100,000) = 0.75.$$

8. Continue to add additional points to the utility function in the same manner. We might, then, say build a function with a number of points as listed below:

Monetary Value(£)	U(M)
-10,000	0
-2,500	0.25
15,000	0.50
47,000	0.75
100,000	1.00

9. If we plot points on the utility function it is possible to assess the general shape of the function and to determine whether the individual is risk neutral, risk adverse, or risk preferring.

You should note that the utility function that we have just constructed depends upon the certainty equivalents selected by the decision maker. A utility function is specific to the individual, and indeed may vary for an individual in different circumstances. Typically individuals have different attitudes to risk associated with money depending upon whether the money is their own personal money, or their employer's money. It is possible to calculate the utility function of a group of people involved in a decision making process, by asking them to arrive at certainty equivalents to given lotteries by consensus. This process, might , for instance, be used to assess the attitude to risk of a group of top managers.

Certainty Equivalents and Risk Premiums

In assessing utility functions above we have used the concept of a certainty equivalent. A certainty equivalent for a lottery can be defined as the certain or sure amount which is equivalent, for a given decision maker to a lottery L, where the lottery L involves some uncertainty. Since many business decisions have an element of uncertainty associated with them certainty equivalents can be a useful concept.

Certainty equivalents have a number of applications in assessing attitudes to risk. The certainty equivalent can, for example, be viewed as the maximum insurance that the decision maker would pay to be freed of an undesirable risk. An alternative interpretation is that the certainty equivalent is the minimum certain amount that one would be willing to accept for selling a desirable, but uncertain set of outcomes. A business may, for example have developed a new product and then be faced with a decision concerning whether to sell the rights to manufacture the product for a specified sum, or to take the gamble of investing more money in production plant and launching the product onto the marketplace. This gamble leaves the company exposed to large risks, but also may potentially lead to large gains.
Certainty equivalents may be calculated by one of two methods: using the utility function, or subjectively.

1. If we already have an appropriate utility function the certainty equivalent can be calculated directly from the utility function. For example, if introducing a new product has utility 0.524, and £17,500 also has utility 0.524 then £17,500 is the certainty equivalent of the new product introduction.
2. The certainty equivalent may be derived subjectively and directly by asking how much a decision maker is prepared to pay to insure against a risk.

Example 9.5

This example demonstrates simply how utility functions and certainty equivalents may be used to calculate the level of insurance premium that is appropriate to cover a perceived level of risk. Suppose a small business has to assess whether or not to insure premises worth £A against a fire that would reduce assets by an amount B. The insurance premium would cost i. The possible strategies, and associated events and their outcomes are summarised below:

	Fire	No Fire
Insure	A - i	A - i
Do not insure	A - B	A

The action taken depends on the probability assigned to the outcome fire. Suppose that this probability is p. If we were to compare the EV of the two strategies we would insure only if:

A - i $\geq$ A - pB

But here EV does not give an appropriate solution. For example, if the property was worth £100,000, the insurance premium could be £200. This would require a probability of at least 1/500 of a fire in any one year for the insurance to be worthwhile. In reality the risk is probably lower than this and thus the individual would not insure. In practice, however, we know that an individual probably would insure. This is because most people are prepared to pay a premium in excess of the monetary value of insurance. This reflects their utility function which shows that individuals may be risk averse when considering insuring significant assets that have taken some while to acquire.

Risk Premiums

Risk premiums are a further measure that can be extracted from a utility function. Suppose an individual has a utility function U(I). The EV of a gamble is I_2 and the certainty equivalent is I*. Note $U(I_2)$ = U (I*).

The difference between the expected value and the certainty equivalent of a gamble i.e. (I_2 - I*) is the risk premium associated with that gamble for that individual. The risk premium measures how much risk aversion there is in a given portion of an individual's utility function. For two people faced with the same gamble, the one with the higher risk premium is more risk averse than the one with a lower risk premium.

Risk premiums for an individual, for a given gamble may vary in different parts of the utility function. They are a useful measure of an individuals attitude to risk.

Conclusion

The application of the expected monetary value criterion does not always lead to the choice of a strategy that a good decision maker would select. In such cases it is asserted that individuals make decisions to maximize expected utility. Utility takes the decision makers attitude to risk into account and is particularly appropriate when major decisions need to be made. Unfortunately utility can be difficult to measure and it may not always be possible to assign a numerical value to utility. In order to be able to compare the utility of different strategies it is necessary to make a number of assumptions concerning a person's attitude to risk, such as, that with any two alternatives it is possible for the decision maker to decide whether they are indifferent between them, or which one they prefer.

Utility functions can be constructed to represent the subjective attitude of a decision maker to risk. The general shape of these utility functions may indicate whether the decision maker is risk averse, risk seeking, or risk neutral. The construction of utility functions requires the use of the concept of a certainty equivalent. A certainty equivalent is the minimum certain amount that a decision maker would be willing to accepts for selling a desirable, but uncertain set of outcomes.

Review Questions

1. Explain why the expected value criterion is not always an appropriate decision criterion. How is the concept of utility useful?
2. What are the main measurement scales that might be considered for measuring utility?
3. Give two key assumptions that underlie utility theory.
4. Draw the utility function of a risk preferring decision maker. How does this function vary from the function of someone who maximised utility by maximising EMV?
5. In what types of situations is utility appropriate?
6. What are the steps in assessing your own utility function?
7. Explain the concept of a certainty equivalent.
8. What applications does the concept of risk premium have?

Case Study Questions

1. Build your own general utility function for values ranging from - £10,00 to £100,000, using the approach outlined earlier in this chapter . Are you generally risk averse or risk preferring?
Now consider the options in terms of:

- risks and ventures using your own personal money;
- risks and ventures using your employer's money;
- Is there a difference in your attitude to risk.?

2. A manager has a utility index of 4 for a loss of £1000, and 10 for a profit of £3000. She says that she is indifferent between £10 for certain and the following lottery:
a 0.3 chance of a £1000 loss and a 0.7 chance of a £3000 profit. What is her utility index for 10?

3. Suppose that you have a personal utility function that can be represented by U(X) = X3/4, where X is in pounds ($0 \leq X \leq 2{,}000$). You are offered the following choices:

- A £8 for certain
- B A lottery with a 0.5 chance of £0 and a 0.5 chance of £64.

Which lottery would you choose?

4. The Bristol Engineering Group has the following utility function when considering bidding for contracts.

$$U(X) = X/100 - 200$$

a. Suppose the company is considering bidding for a given contract. It will cost £2,000 to prepare the bid. If the bid is lost this cost will also be lost. If the bid is won, the company will make £40,000 and recover the bid cost. Suppose the company believes that the probability of winning the contract is 0.5 if a bid is submitted. What should it do?

b. What would the probability of winning have to be before the company should submit a bid?

c. Comment upon the utility function for the company.

5. The following table summarises the risks where an organisation would consider insurance and the maximum annual premium that the organisation is prepared to pay for that insurance. The organisation has assets of £15 million.

Incident	Loss	Probability	Max. Annual Premium
small fire	0.5	.005	3500
explosion	1.0	.001	1300
large fire	4.0	.005	28000
supplier strike	1.5	.101	18000
internal strike	2.0	.010	24000

If we take the utility of the current assets to be 1.00, work out the other points on the utility function associated with each of the certainty equivalents given in the table, and plot the utility curve.

10

Other Decision Making Techniques

Objectives

When you have read this chapter you should have a general appreciation of the nature of a wide variety of model building techniques and the circumstances in which you might find them useful. More specifically you will have an appreciation of the value of the following model building techniques:

- Simulation
- Linear Programming
- Other Mathematical Programming Techniques
- Inventory Models
- Queuing Models
- Critical Path Models

Introduction

This chapter is intended to briefly review some of the other decision making techniques that there has not been the opportunity to explore in any depth, in order that the reader has some awareness of their existence and may be able to identify a problem in which they might be applied.

It is useful to start such an overview as this by reviewing the basic classification of models that was originally offered in Chapter 6. Recall that we identified three types of problems: simple problems, complex problems and dynamic problems. The intervening chapters have considered some of the key techniques for dealing with simple problems. Here we briefly examine some of the techniques associated with the solution of complex and dynamic problems. To explore these techniques further you will need to read other texts which deal with the techniques in detail. Our primary objective here is to introduce the nature of these techniques, so that the reader is aware of their existence and when such a technique might prove useful.

Simulation

Any model building process is a form of simulation. The model is used to simulate a set of conditions or a process. Simulating is the act of experimenting with a model and observing the consequences. A town planner who makes a scale model of a proposed development and moves the buildings into different patterns to achieve the best arrangement is performing a simulation.

However, in decision theory, the term simulation has a more closely defined meaning. Simulation models are usually built to deal with problems that involve relatively complex situations with a large number of variables and relationships. A simulation model may be used for one of three reasons:

- the model involves many variables and relationships;
- the relationships between the variables are not well understood by the decision maker and cannot therefore be represented by mathematical equalities or inequalities;
- although a situation may be capable of being represented by a series of mathematical equalities and inequalities, these expressions have no mathematical solution.

The techniques described elsewhere in this text are primarily analytical, such that mathematical solutions are possible, but there are many problems that are not amenable to such approaches. Typical business examples are: most queuing systems other than the very simplest; inventory control situations; production planning problems; and business planning. By means of simulation the behaviour of a system can be observed over a period of time. Thus, for example, the simulation of an inventory system over two years could be carried out using a simulation model on a computer in a few minutes. In addition the analyst can experiment with the system, by, for example, altering the frequencies of receipts and issues, the decision rules governing the re-order levels and the re-order quantities, to observe the effects of these changes on the system being simulated.

Simulation can be used for ascertaining and designing control mechanisms for existing systems, or for studying complex situations and noting the effect of changes to some of the variables. In addition, simulation may offer an insight into a proposed system. Simulation models have a further advantage over other analytical techniques. Simulation relies upon an understanding of the structure of a situation, and appropriate identification of variables and their relationships, rather than on what some might regard as abstruse mathematical techniques. This is more consistent with the managers approach to decision making.

Simulation can be used to model a variety of different kinds of situations. For example, in models for financial and business modelling, a computer model of the financial structure of the business is stored, and the user is able to interact with the computer and explore the effects of various financial strategies with the aid of the model. Models based on business games may be used to examine the competitive forces in a marketplace. Such models can also be used in training since they permit experimentation without the cost of mistakes.

Many simulation models deal with situations where there is uncertainty, and events may occur according to some probability distribution. Often the number of possible combinations of events prohibits the computation of all possible outcomes. The type of simulation models that deal with uncertainty are referred to as Monte Carlo simulation. In such situations simulation models operate by effectively running a series of events and observing the outcome of a sufficiently large number of events. Suppose, for instance, we wished to model work flow through a production unit, where units for processing appear at the production unit, possibly as the result of orders, unpredictability and at random. The simulation model would run through a number of occurrences of the appearance of items for production, and by analysing how these trials are distributed over time it is possible to learn, for example, what the maximum waiting time for an order might be, or what the average waiting time for an order is. It is also possible by changing some of the parameters of the model to investigate how the situation might be improved in some sense. In order for this model to work it is necessary to have some mechanism to determine when orders will arrive for processing. If we assume that orders arrive at random, then we need a mechanism for generating random numbers. Computer based models generate pseudo random numbers using a random number generating device. Computer based simulation models were a relatively early application of computers in decision making, because simulation models requires that a large number of trials be run. These are much more easily handled in computer based models.

Linear Programming

Linear programming (LP) is a widely used technique that can be applied to determine the best decision even in situations where there are thousands of variables and relationships to consider.

Elements of the LP Model

All LP models are essentially of the same form:

There are decision variables, $X_1, X_2...,X_n$

We seek to maximize an objective function, expressed as:

$$f = c_1X_1 + c_2X_2 + ... c_nX_n$$

where c_i f_i are constants determined by the relationships between the variables in the decision situation.

Relationships between the variables or constraints can be expressed in the form of linear inequalities or equalities, i.e.

$$a_1X_1 + a_2X_2 ...+ a_nX_n = b \quad \text{or}$$
$$a_1X_1 + a_2X_2 ...+ a_nX_n \geq b$$

where the a_i's are constants and b is a constant.

A solution is the set of values of the decision variables that achieves the desired maximum or minimum within the various constraints.

Example 10.1

A company manufactures two products A and B. The per unit profit for each of the two products is summarised in the table below:

Product	Per unit profit
A	5
B	2

The company must decide how many of each product to manufacture, given that there are other constraints, such as which machines can manufacture which of A and B, and the availability of skilled staff, which constrain the company from merely manufacturing as many of product B as possible. Clearly overall B can make more profit than A, if the choice is between making A or B.

In a linear programming model this problem will be expressed in terms of attempting to maximize an objective function, such as:

$$f = 5X_1 + 2X_2$$

where X_1 is the number of units of A to be manufactured, and X_2 is the number of units of B to be manufactured; f is the profit.

This objective function must be maximised within constraints imposed by the resources available to the manager.

However, if the situation is more complex and the plant makes 20 different products in 15 different departments, and each product requires a different production time in each department, and each department contains 10 processes, and each product requires different production time in each process, the solution is far from obvious. We need some assistance in determining the optimum product mix. Linear programming is ideal for this kind of problem.

Examples of Application Areas

Linear Programming has a number of applications. Examples are:

- product mix;
- transportation — identification of the optimum mix of routes.
- scheduling of production.

In practice, in order to solve these kinds of problems computer software designed to assist with LP problems will be enlisted.

Other Mathematical Programming Techniques

The form of the linear programming model needs some modification to deal with situations where some of its assumptions do not allow for accurate modelling of the decision situation. Other techniques that have been developed include:

1. *Integer programming,* which is similar to linear programming but ensures that the answers are integers. For example a linear programming analysis might recommend that you make 8.42 trucks. Integer programming will give an integer number of trucks say 8 or 9. In some situations it is sufficient to round a number offered by a linear programming model, but in others this solution can be wrong.

2. *Linear Programming with Uncertainty*, or chance constrained programming, deals with LP in situations where there is uncertainty concerning the values taken by some of the variables.

3. *Non-linear programming,* deals with non-linear problems. In these the objective function or constraints are not linearly related to the variables.

4. *Dynamic programming* covers situations where there is a series of related decisions to make, and the outcome of one decision may affect the nature of the second, and so on.

Inventory Models

Inventory control has been very satisfactorily treated by quantitative methods. In an ongoing inventory control system there are two decisions to be made:

1. When to place an order — i.e. identification of the optimum order point, so that when the inventory level falls to the order point, we place a replenishment order. This assumes that the order point is determined by the units in store, rather than the passage of time (placing an order each month, for example).

2. The size of the order — i.e. how many units should be ordered in order to minimise the cost associated with maintaining an inventory.

In the simple case, demand is assumed to be constant. Here there are two general types of costs to be considered:

- the cost of placing an order;
- the cost of carrying inventory in stock.

The optimum order size and optimum order point will, in general, be a function of these two costs plus the intensity or rate of use.

ABC Analysis

ABC Analysis is a useful preliminary to the construction of an inventory control model. In a situation where the inventory consists of a large number of items (which it usually does), it is useful to identify those items that are most crucial, and whose inventory must be controlled. In order to do this items can be ranked according to some performance measure that reflects their importance. A common measure that is used is the annual sales for each item, although this is only directly applicable in a sales or end-product situation and not a raw materials situation.

The ABC analysis is achieved by plotting an ABC curve, which ranks each item by its sales in monetary terms, and then plotting the cumulative sales versus the number of different items in the inventory. The curve can be divided into three regions:

- A items — which account for the top 50 percent of sales;
- C items — which account for the bottom 50 per cent of sales;
- B items — the items in between.

Then, A items should receive the most analysis, monitoring and review, with B items receiving some attention and C items can be managed more casually.

Economic Order Quantity with Known Demand

As indicated above the simplest situation is when the demand is known and constant. In this situation the optimum order size can be calculated by analysing total costs. The total cost for a given period will be equal to the sum of the ordering costs plus the costs of carrying inventory during the period. Assume that the units will be received all at once:

Let:
K = incremental cost of placing an order
k_c = annual cost of carrying one unit of inventory D = annual total usage (demand) in units
Q = optimum order size in units (the unknown)
Note
D/Q = annual number of orders
$Q/2$ = average inventory (assuming linear usage)

Then

Q ($k_c/2$) = annual cost of carrying inventory
D (K/Q) = annual cost of placing orders
Then total annual cost is

$$Q (k_c/2) + D (K/Q)$$

The minimum total cost occurs when the costs of the two components are equal and opposite in sign. Using this we can obtain a formula for the optimal order quantity Q. At the optimum:

$$Q (k_c/2) = D (K/Q)$$
and
$$Q = \sqrt{\frac{2KD}{k_c}}$$

This is referred to as the EOQ (economic order quantity) formula.

This simple case of inventory control illustrates the principles upon which other models are built. There are a number of variations on this simple model that it may be necessary to accommodate.

Other Inventory Control Models

First there are some simple changes to the model that still assume known demand. For example we might consider:

- quantity discounts, which will tend to be incremental in nature.
- a continuous flow of product, where instead of receiving all items ordered at once, items may be received over a period of time, either individually, or in small batches.

Next, models must take into account where demand is uncertain. These again can be divided into two categories. Models where reordering is possible and those where it is not.

When reordering is possible we can continue to use the EOQ formula for order size, but assessing the order point is more complex. This needs to take into account the fact that we do not have precise information about when we will run out, only probabilistic information. Necessarily this means that on some occasions we will run out of stock. In such circumstances we need also to take into account the shortage cost, or alternatively, to specify a desired level of service. Models of this kind are only appropriate when demand comes from a reasonably large number of independent sources. Where these models can not be applied, as in a raw materials situation, a technique known as material requirements planning may be applied.

The last category of models deal with inventory control with uncertainty and no reordering. These are one shot situations where there is no opportunity for reordering and the item cannot be stored for future orders. Here we are faced only with the problem of how much should be ordered if we are faced with demand with known probabilities and reordering is not possible.

Queuing Models

Queues or waiting lines are too common in life. Typically models that deal with queues are concerned with processes characterised by random arrivals (i.e. arrivals at random time intervals); the servicing of customers is also a random process. If we assume that there are costs of waiting in line and if there are costs of adding more channels (i.e. more service facilities) we seek to minimise the sum of the costs of waiting and the costs of providing service facilities. The computations will lead to such measures as the expected number of people in line, the expected waiting time of the arrivals, and the expected percentage utilisation of the service facilities. These measures can then be used in the cost computations to determine the number and capacity of service facilities that are desirable.

Typical applications for queuing theory might be to determine the optimum number of:

- toll booths for a bridge;
- doctors available for clinic;
- repair persons servicing machines;
- landing strips for aircraft.

Many queuing problems can be solved on the basis of past experience of demand, and the manager can effectively apply intuition. Where the situation is too complex or new, mathematical models of queuing can be useful. There are a number of different models of the queuing situation which cater for the different kinds of queuing situation. These are defined by the variability in the major elements of any queuing situation. These are:

1. *Arrivals*
Customers come into the system for service. They may come singly or in batches; they may come evenly spaced in time or in a random pattern; they may come from an infinite (very large) population of possible arrivals (e.g. all the people in a city) or from a finite set (e.g. one of ten machines that might break down).

2. *Services*
Each customer must be served. The length of time that it takes to complete a service is an important element. It may take the same time for each customer, or service times may vary in a random fashion.

3. *Number of Servers*
There may be only one server channel, or many. A customer may need only

to be processed by one server, or may need to be processed by several in turn. Servers may have different service rates.

4. *Queue Discipline*

While customers wait for service they are in a queue. They may be served according to different rules. There may be only one queue, or separate queues for each server. There may be a space limit on the queue, and customers who arrive when the queue is full may turn away (Balk). The order in which customers are served is often FIFO (First in - first out), but other priority systems may operate.

5. *Measures of Performance*

there are a number of different measures that can be adopted as a measure of how well a queuing situation is performing. Generally the time customers spend waiting is important, and we may look at the average waiting time. The average number of customers in the queue and the cost of operating the system may also be important. These measures would be used to determine the optimum number of servers and capacity of the queuing system.

Critical Path Models

Critical path models and PERT (Program Evaluation and Review Technique) are used to manage the planning and control of major projects with many separate activities that require co-ordination. Often these activities must be performed in a specific sequence in order to accomplish some major project, although some of the activities must proceed in series and others proceed in parallel. The technique allows a manager to calculate the expected total amount of time that the project will take to complete, and highlights the bottleneck activities in the project so that the manager may either allocate more resources to them or monitor them carefully. The technique needs to cater with both known and uncertain activity times.

In order to apply the technique it is necessary to know for each activity in the project:

- the sequencing requirements
- an estimate of the time that each activity will take.

We then draw a network diagram of the project, showing the activities, and their sequence. Associated with each activity is its time.

A path is defined as a sequence of connected activities in the project. We identify all of the paths on the network, and work out their lengths in time. A longest path is described as a critical path. The length of a critical path determines the minimum time in which the project can be completed. The activities on a critical path are the bottleneck activities in the project, i.e. those activities that have the potential to hold the project up. A critical path is important, since the project can only be completed in less time if one of the activities on a critical path can have its time reduced. Also any delays in activities on a critical path will produce delays in the completion of the project.

In simple problems a critical path can be found by inspection of the network diagram. In projects involving many hundreds of activities, a technique for the identification of a critical path is valuable. This is based on the calculation of the Early Start (ES), Late Start(LS) and Early Finish(EF) and Late Finish(LF) times for each activity. The ES and EF times are obtained by working through the network, starting from the first task. For each activity, ES is the largest of the EF times for all preceding activities, and EF is the ES plus the time for the activity itself. The EF of the last task is the minimum project completion time.

The LS and LF times are obtained by working backward through the network. For each activity, the LS is the LF minus the activity time, and the LF is the smallest LS of immediate successor activities. Slack time is the difference between ES and LS for each activity. Activities with zero slack time are on a critical path.

Management may choose to allocate additional resources and incur additional costs to reduce total project time. By selectively reducing the time for critical path activities with the smallest incremental cost, the optimal trade-off function relating project time and project cost can be developed.

If the activity times in the network are uncertain, then the length of a critical path needs to be calculated using the probability distribution of the actual project time, and the probability that each activity will be on a critical path can be obtained by simulation.

The PERT technique forces the planner to specify the activities that constitute the project, and to estimate their times and to specify their sequencing requirements. The construction of the network diagram can in itself pinpoint major problems in the project. If a critical path is longer than desired, then resources can be re-allocated.

Conclusion

There are a number of different mathematical model building techniques, each of which has been designed to solve a different set of problems. Some of the key techniques are: simulation, linear programming, other mathematical programming techniques, inventory models, queuing models and critical path models. It is important to appreciate when each of these techniques might assist in the solution of a business problem.

Review Questions

1. Explain when simulation models might be useful.
2. Give some examples of situations in which you might make use of linear programming.
3. What is the difference between linear programming and non-linear

programming. Try to give an example that demonstrates when you would use each.

4. What is the primary objective of inventory control models?
5. Explain the concept of Economic Order Quantity.
6. When might you use ABC analysis?
7. Identify some variations on the basic inventory control model.
8. What are the major elements of any queuing situation?
9. List some types of queue discipline with which you are familiar. Give examples of where you have seen each in operation.
10. What benefits do critical path models offer in the management and control of major projects?
11. Explain the concept of critical path.

Answers to Numerical Case Study Questions

Chapter 6

Variables
PAPER COST (£ per rem)
EDITORIAL COST(£ per hour)
PRINTING COST(£ per issue)
TYPESETTING COST(£ per issue)
SUBSCRIPTION COST (£ per copy)
ADVERTISING RATE (£ per page)
DISTRIBUTION COST (£ per issue per copy)
NUMBER OF PAGES ADVERTISING
NUMBER OF SOLD SUBSCRIPTIONS
NUMBER OF MEMBER SUBSCRIPTIONS
NUMBER OF HOURS EDITORIAL WORK (hours per issue)
NUMBER OF ISSUES PER YEAR

Intermediate Variables

SUBSCRIPTION REVENUE
ADVERTISING REVENUE
All annual costs listed below.

Relationships

ANNUAL PROFIT + ANNUAL REVENUE - ANNUAL EXPENSE

ANNUAL EXPENSE = ANNUAL PAPER COST + ANNUAL EDITORIAL COST + ANNUAL PRINTING COST + ANNUAL TYPESETTING COST + ANNUAL DISTRIBUTION COST + ANNUAL ADVERTISING COST

ANNUAL REVENUE = SUBSCRIPTION REVENUE + ADVERTISING REVENUE.

ANNUAL ADVERTISING REVENUE + NUMBER OF PAGES ADVERTISING x ADVERTISING RATE

SUBSCRIPTION REVENUE = NUMBER OF SOLD SUBSCRIPTIONS x SUBSCRIPTION COST

ANNUAL PAPER COST = NUMBER OF SHEETS USED IN EACH ISSUE x COST PER SHEET x NUMBER OF ISSUES.

ANNUAL PRINTING COST = PRINTING COST x NUMBER OF ISSUES

ANNUAL TYPESETTING COST = TYPESETTING COST x NUMBER OF ISSUES

ANNUAL DISTRIBUTION COST = DISTRIBUTION COST x NUMBER OF ISSUES x NUMBER OF COPIES.

NUMBER OF COPIES = NUMBER OF SOLD SUBSCRIPTIONS + NUMBER OF MEMBER SUBSCRIPTIONS.

ANNUAL ADVERTISING COST = 0.10 x ANNUAL ADVERTISING REVENUE.

Chapter 7

Decision Criteria

1. (a) d_6, with a value of 3.75
    (b) d_1, d_4, d_6, since they all have minimum profits of 0
    (c) d_5 for which the value is 5
    (d) d_4 with an expected value of 3.4
    (e) d_4 and d_6 dominate d_1 by outcome dominance
    (f) d_4 dominates d_3 by event dominance. Also, d_4 and d_6 dominate d_1 by event dominance, since they dominate by outcome dominance.
    (g) It is necessary to develop a table showing cumulative probabilities for each of d_2, d_4, d_5 and d_6. We should not consider d_1 and d_3 since they are dominated by outcome or event dominance. d_4, d_5, d_6 dominate d_2. d_4 dominates d_5 .
    (h) d_4 and d_6 are undominated.

4. (a) Outcome or event dominance can not be used because the outcomes are all the same. Only the probabilities are different, so probabilistic dominance must be used.

The following table can be created:

Payoff	A		B		C	
	P(X)	(P X or more)	P(X)	P(X or more)	P(X)	P(X or more)
-50	0.4	1.0	0.2	1.0	0.2	1.0
0	0.0	0.6	0.0	0.8	0.1	0.8
50	0.4	0.6	0.2	0.8	0.1	0.7
100	0.2	0.2	0.4	0.6	0.6	0.6
150	0.0	0.0	0.2	0.2	0.0	0.0

P(X or more) is always at least as large for B as for C, so B dominates C by probabilistic dominance.

(b) The expected value of each option, A, B and C can be calculated. The values are:

$EV(A) = 30, EV(B) = 70, EV(C) = 55$
Using the expected value criterion we would choose B.

5. Expected value is calculated thus: The table shows the costs per kilogram of beans.

Season	Probability(P)	Buy Now(X_1)	P(X_1)	Buy Later(X_2)	P(X_2)	Buy Half(X_3)	P(X_3)
Good	0.3	20	6	12	3.6	16	4.8
Fair	0.4	20	8	22	8.8	21	8.4
Poor	0.3	20	6	28	8.4	24	7.2
EV		20		20.8		20.4	

The company would decide to buy later under the Expected Value criterion.

Under the Minimax criterion , where we examine the maximum possible price for each decision and find the smallest, the chosen decision would be : Buy Now.

Probability

1. (a) P(under 55) = 9/30 = 0.30. This is a marginal or simple probability.
   (b) P(55 or older/ Marketing) = 5/30 = 0/167. This is a joint probability
   (c) P(under 55 / Finance) = 4/18 = 0.222. This is a conditional probability
   (d) No, because P(under 55) does not equal P(under 55/ Finance) which would be necessary for independence.

2. Since daily demand is independent:
   (a) 10 requests   P(5 AND 5) = 0.3 x 0.3 = 0.09
   (b) 11 requests   P(5 AND 6) = 0.3 x 0.7 = 0.21
                       P(6 AND 5) = 0.7 x 0.3 = 0.21
                       0.21 + 0.21 = 0.42
   (c) 12 requests   P(6 AND 6) = 0.7 x 0.7 = 0.49

Expected Values

1. Event(X_i)	Probability of Event(P (X_i))	$X_i P(X_i)$
.01	.10	.001
.02	.15	.003
.03	.20	.006

.....*continued*

1. | Event(X_i) | Probability of Event($P(X_i)$) | $X_iP(X_i)$ |
|---|---|---|
| .04 | .30 | .012 |
| .05 | .20 | .010 |
| .10 | .03 | .003 |
| .15 | .02 | .003 |
| Expected Value | | .038 |

2. | Event | Fraction of Hour Worked(X_i) | Probability of Event($P(X_i)$) | $X_iP(X_i)$ |
|---|---|---|---|
| Heavy rain | 0.0 | 0.2 | 0.0 |
| Light | 0.5 | 0.3 | 0.15 |
| Dry | 1.0 | 0.5 | 0.50 |
| Expected Value of Faction of Hour Worked | | | 0.65 |

Time taken = 65/0.65 = 100 hours.

3. | Probability $P(X_i)$) | Demand (X_i) | $X_iP(X_i)$) |
|---|---|---|
| 0.1 | 50 | 5 |
| 0.3 | 100 | 30 |
| 0.3 | 150 | 4 |
| 0.15 | 200 | 30 |
| 0.10 | 250 | 25 |
| 0.05 | 300 | 15 |
| Expected Value = | | 150 |

Expected Profit is 150 x 50 = £7500
Total expected profit = Expected profit - Introduction Costs = £7500 - £5000
= £2500

Chapter 8
1 (a)

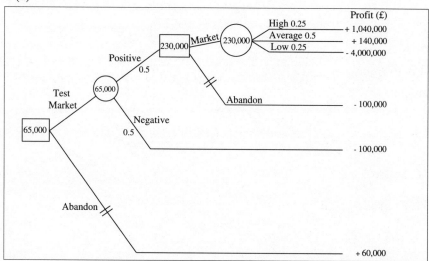

(b) Decision 2

EV (Market) = (0.25 x £1040,000) = (0.5 x £140,000) + (0.25 x -£400,000)
= £230,000

EV (Abandon) = -£100,000

Therefore the company should decide to market the product.

Decision 1

EV(Test Market) = (0.5 x £230,000) + (0.5 x -£100,000) = £65,000

EV(Give UP) = £60,000

On the basis of the EV value, the company should test market and if this is positive market nationally.

(c) The choice at Decision 1 is between £65000 on a gamble, if they Test Market, and £60,000 for certain if they abandon the product. Given that there are many assumptions and simplifications involved in this model the sensible decision maker may seek more accurate information, or, if this is not available, would probably choose the less risky option and give up the project.

2. (a)

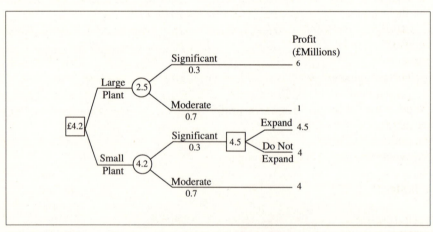

(b) The company should build the small plant and expand it if the promotion effort captures a significant share of the market. The expected net profit is £4.2 million.

3. (a)

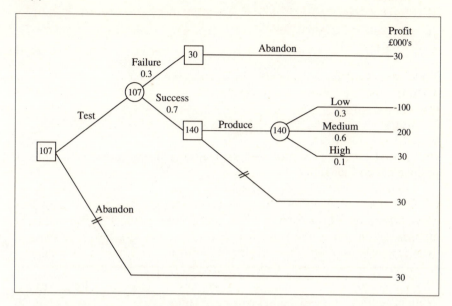

(b) Expected value decision rule gives the following result: Company should test the product. The Expected Net Profit is £107,000.
It is also possible to evaluate the options using the minimax or equally likely decision criteria.

(c) There are a number of assumptions and estimates, including:

the estimates of the conditional profits
the estimates of the probabilities
the options available to the company
the events that may befall the company.

Chapter 9

2. $U(-1000) = 4$
   $U(3000) = 10$

   $U(10) = 0.3U(-1000) + 0.7U(3000)$
   $ = 0.3 \times 4 + 0.7 \times 10$
   $ = 1.2 + 7.0$
   $ = 8.2$

3. $U(X) = 3X/4$
   $U(8) = 3 \times 8 /4 = 6$
   $U(\text{Lottery B}) = 0.5U(0) + 0.5\ U(64)$
   $\phantom{U(\text{Lottery B})} = 0.5\ (3 \times 0 /4) + 0.5 (3 \times 64/ 4)$
   $\phantom{U(\text{Lottery B})} = 24$

On this basis you should choose lottery B.

4. U(X) = X/100 - 200
(a) Alternative 1: Do not bid
U(0) = -200

Alternative 2 : Bid
U(Bid) = 0.5 U(-2000) + 0.5U(40000)
     = 0.5(-220) + 0.5(200)
     = -10

Therefore U(Bid) > U(No Bid) and the company should Bid.

(b) Let p be the probability of winning the bid. Then:

(1-p) (-220) + p(200) = -200
420p = 20
p = 1/21

The probability of success has to be fairly low to make it worthwhile to bid. With this utility function the bid looks very attractive.

5. Each item in this table may provide a point on the utility curve. The first incident implies:

0.005 U(15 - 0.5) + 0.995U(15) = U(15 - 0.0035)
or 0.005U(14.5) + (0.995)(0.6) = 0.375 + (14.9965)(0.015)

since the utility on the right hand side of the equation falls within the linear range. We have then:

U(14.5) = 0.5895.

Similar equations yield the utilities for the other points and the utility function may be plotted.

Readings

Alter, S | Decision support systems: current practice and continuing challenges.- *Reading, MA*: Addison-Wesley, 1980

Avison, D E and Fitzgerald | *Information systems development: methodologies, techniques and tools.-* Oxford: Blackwell Scientific Publications, 1988

Bierman, H et al | *Quantitative analysis for business decisions.-* 8th edition. Homewood, Il: Irwin, 1991

Braancheau, J and Wetherbe, J C | Key information system issues. - *MIS Quarterly*, 11 March 1987, 23-46

Carr, H H | *Managing end-user computing.* Prentice Hall, 1988

Cash, J et al | *Corporate information systems management:text and cases.-* 2nd edition.- Irwin Homewood, 1988

Cash, J et al | *Corporate information systems management: the issues facing senior executives* - 2nd ed.- Homewood, Il:Irwin, 1988

Checkland, P | *Systems thinking, systems practice.-* Wiley, 1981

Curtis, G | *Business information systems: analysis, design and practice.-* Wokingham: Addison-Wesley, 1989

Curwin, R and Slater, R | *Quantitative methods for business decisions.-* Chapman and Hall, 1988

Dans, G B and Olson, M H | *Management information systems.* - 2nd edition.- Addison-Wesley, 1991

Davis, G B and Olson, M H | *Management information systems: Conceptual foundations, structure and development.-* 2nd ed.- New York: McGraw-Hill, 1985

Earl, M J	Competitive advantage through information technology: eight maxims for senior managers. *Journal of Multinational Business*, Summer 1988
Earl, M J	*Information management: the strategic dimension.-* Oxford University Press, 1988
Ginzberg, M J et al (eds)	*Decision support systems.-* New York: Elsevier, 1982
Gordon, G et al	*Quantitative decision making for business.* - 3rd edition. - Prentice Hall, 1990
Gorry, G A and Scott-Morton, M S	A framework for management information systems. *Sloan Management Review*, 13(1), 55-70
Gregory, G	*Decision analysis.* - New York, London: Plenum Press, 1988
Gummesson, E	*Qualitative methods in management research.-* Chartwell Bratt, 1988
Hanke, J et al	*Statistical decision making models for management.-* Allyn and Bacon, 1984
Harmon, P and King, D	*Expert systems: artifical intelligence in business.-* New York: Wiley, 1985
King, W	Strategic planning for management information systems. *MIS Quarterly* 2(1), March 1978, 27-37
Kroenke, D	*Management information systems.-* McGraw Hill, 1989
Lucey, T	*Quantitative Techniques.* - 4th edition.- London:DP Publications, 1992
Lucey, T	*Management information systems.-* 6th edition.- DP Publications, 1991
McFarlan, F W	Information technology changes the way you compete. *Harvard Business Review,* May-June 1984
McKeown, P G and Leitch, R A	*Management information systems: managing withcomputers.-* Fort Worth: Dryden Press, 1993
Panko, R R	*End user computing.-* Wiley, 1988
Parsaye, K and Chignell, M	*Expert systems for experts.-* Wiley, 1988

Patching, K   *The information centre, managing the growth of end-user
                          computing for corporate advantage.-* Quiller Press, 1989

Porter, M E and   *How information gives you competitive advantage.*
Millar, V E   *Harvard Business Review,* July- August 1985

Quinn, J B et al   *The strategic process, concepts, context and cases.-*
                          Prentice Hall, 1988

Remenyi, D S J   *Introducing Strategic Information Systems Planning.-*
                          Manchester: NCC Blackwell, 1991

Remenyi, D S J   *Strategic information systems - development,
                          implementation, case studies.-* NCC Blackwell, 1989

Rockart, J F   Chief executives define their own data needs. *Harvard
                          Business Review*, Mar/Apr, 1979

Sanders, D H   *Computers today.-* 3rd ed.- New York: McGraw-Hill,
                          1988

Scott, G M   *Principles of management information systems.-*
                          McGraw Hill, 1986

Senn, J A   *Information systems in management.* - 4th edition.-
                          Wadsworth, 1990

Senn, J A and   Corporate strategy and the information resource:
Wilkes, R E   confronting the issues. *Proceedings of Joint International
                          Symposium On Information Systems* (Sydney, Australia:
                          Australian Computer Society), 1988, 165-187

Shank, M E et al   Critical success factor analysis as a methodology for
                          MIS planning.- *MIS Quarterly* 9(2), June 1985

Silverman, B G, ed   Expert systems for business.- *Reading, MA*: Addison-
                          Wesley, 1987

Thirkettle, G I   *Business statistics.* - 9th edition.- Pitman, 1991
and Wheldon, S

Turban, E   *Decision support systems, a managerial perspective.-*
                          Macmillan, 1988

Ward, J et al   *Strategic planning for information systems.-* Chichester:
                          Wiley, 1990

References

Ackoff, R L   Management misinformation systems.- *Management Science* 14,(4), December 1967, B140-156

March, J G and   *Organisations.-* New York: Wiley, 1958
Simon, H A

Rockart, J F and   *Executive support systems.-* Homewood, Illinois:Irwin, 1988.

DeLong, D W   *The new science of management decision.-* New York:
Simon, H A   Harper&Row, 1960.- revised ed. Englewood
                   Cliffs,NJ:Prentice Hall, 1977

Index